AWAKENING LOVE'S VIBRATIONS

An Artist's Search
Takes You on a Journey
to Explore the Esoteric Arts,
the Wisdom of her Spiritual Teachers,
and Travel to Mayan and other Ancient Sites.

Book Two: A Spiritual Journey Trilogy
Irene Vincent

Black & White Edition
93 Images

Sun Door

AWAKENING LOVE'S VIBRATIONS

First Published in 2018
Sun Door
1827 Van Ness St.
Port Townsend, WA 98368

Copyright 2018 by Irene Vincent.

All Rights Reserved. No part of this book maybe reproduced or transmitted in any form or by any means, electronic or mechanical, including photocopying, recording, or in any information storage and retrieval system without written permission from the author, except in the case of brief quotations embodied in critical reviews and articles.

ISBN: 978-0-9853980-1-9

LCCN: 2018907849

1. Religion & Spirituality   2. Mind, Body, and Spirit   3. Art   4. Dreams   5. Visions   6. Travel   7. Hinduism   8. Esoteric Arts   9. Symbolism   10. Mayan Ruins   11. Memoir   12. Irene Vincent   13. Non-fiction   14. Adventure

Book Cover Design: Irene Vincent   website: www.irenevincent.com

Cover Art: Irene Vincent, Photo of Irene hiking on Huayna Picchu, Peru

*This book is dedicated
to my family,
to all my spiritual teachers,
to all my friends
and
to all the creative and adventurous souls seeking
to "know thyself."*

Table of Contents

List of Illustrations   vii

Introduction   xi

Chapter One: Pushing Back the Illusions of Darkness   1

Chapter Two: From Politics to Prayer: Missile Totem   5

Chapter Three: From the Ghetto to New Meadow   13

Chapter Four: Maps and Red Flags   19

Chapter Five: Swami Sivananda Radha: A Heart of Love   21

Chapter Six: The Healing Power of "The Divine Light Invocation"   27

Chapter Seven: Trip to Swami Radha's Ashram   33

Chapter Eight: Seeking Essences of Spirit   35

Chapter Nine: Delving into Dreams   39

Chapter Ten: The Mayan Ruins   43

Chapter Eleven: Dreaming and The Dalai Lama Initiation   49

Chapter Twelve: Trip to Esalen for Psychosynthesis   53

Chapter Thirteen: Exploring Shamanism in my Art   57

Chapter Fourteen: Orange County Center for Contemporary Art 1985-87   65

Chapter Fifteen: *Missile Totem of the Ejecting Heart* Transforms Itself   67

Chapter Sixteen: Meeting Swami Vishnudevanand of Allahabad, India   71

Chapter Seventeen: *Seeking Oneness* & *Oneness in Thought*   75

Chapter Eighteen: The Unexpected Trip to Thailand   81

Chapter Nineteen: "Good News, Bad News, What's the Difference?"   87

Chapter Twenty: Mayan Goddess Sculptures   91

Chapter Twenty-one: Mayan Ruins: Tikal, Guatemala   93

Chapter Twenty-two: The Shaman Healing Dream   99

Chapter Twenty-three: Adventures in Peru and Bolivia   101

Chapter Twenty-four: The Cat's Dream Comes True   111

Chapter Twenty-five: Being Healed by Light and Yoga   115

Chapter Twenty-six: Feeling Abundant and The Astrologer   117

Chapter Twenty-seven: What's Up with Peace?   121

Chapter Twenty-eight: Studying Esoteric Ways with Karl Wolf   123

Chapter Twenty-nine: The Hero's Journey / Pivotal Dreams   127

Chapter Thirty: Swami Vishnudevanand Visits in May and Late July   131

Chapter Thirty-one: Not So Easy, Along with Some Good Chapter   133

Thirty-two: Swami Sahajananda Visits during the Breakup Chapter   137

Thirty-three: Oaxaca and the Spiritual Dilemma   141

Chapter Thirty-four: Off to Villahermosa, Palenque, Bonampak, and Yaxchilan   149

Chapter Thirty-five: The Phoenix: *Bird and Snake Singing to the Stars*   157

Third Book & Epilogue   161

About the Author   163

Acknowledgements   170

Questions for You & Book Clubs   171

List of Illustrations

Fig. 1 In 1984, Irene is posing in front of *Journey of the Soul*. 1984, acrylic paint, cheese cloth, and paper on raw canvas, 65"H x 92 ½"W x

Fig. 2 Irene Vincent, sculpture, front side view on base - *Cat Man Pushing Back the Illusions of Darkness*, 1984, acrylic paint on carved plaster, mixed media, cheesecloth, wood etc., 71"H x 34"W x 30"L 3

Fig. 3 Irene Vincent, sculpture without pedestal, back side view - *Cat Man Pushing Back the Illusions of Darkness*, 1984, acrylic paint on carved plaster, mixed media, cheesecloth, wood etc. 3

Fig. 4 Irene Vincent, *Missiles and Coffee Cups*, 1983 Size: 50"H x 72"W 6

Fig. 5 Irene is posing while sculpting *Missile Totem* in her warehouse studio, 1984. 8

Fig. 6 Left - Irene is posing with *Missile Totem* in 1984. 8

Fig. 7 Right – Irene is painting the first layer of red on *Missile Totem* in her warehouse studio 8

Fig. 8 - Irene Vincent - The first view of three sides of *Missile Totem* is a four-breasted masked woman, which implies too many emotions, thus imbalance. She represents third world countries. 1984 10

Fig. 9 – Irene Vincent - The second view of *Missile Totem* is an image of the former Soviet Leader, Leonid Brezhnev, representing Russia. It depicts that power ruled by too much logic and not enough heart is out of balance." 11

Fig. 10 – Irene Vincent - The third view of *Missile Totem* is an image of the former United States President, Ronald Reagan, also meaning that power ruled by too much logic, not enough heart is out of balance." 12

Fig. 11 Irene, Swami Radha, and Robert are having breakfast at 11 New Meadow. 22

Fig. 12 Swami Radha visits. 22

Fig. 13 Swami Radha and I are in my backyard. 22

Fig. 14 Swami Radha 31

Fig. 15 Don Gamble, Irene Vincent, Swami Radha, and Terrence Buie at the Ritz Carlton in Dana Point, CA 32

Fig. 16 Irene and Swami Sahajananda are in Laguna Beach, CA 35

Fig. 17 Irene and Swami Sahajananda are at the Self-Realization Fellowship Lake Shrine Temple. 36

Fig. 18 Irene is in a purple skirt, standing atop Temple of the Warriors, near Chac Mool with serpent heads behind her. Chichen Itza, Mexico 42

Fig. 19 Robert is standing atop the Jaguar and Eagle Temple with the Temple of Kukulkan in the distance. Chichen Itza pyramids, Yucatan, Mexico in 1987. 42

Fig. 20 Chac Mool in Chichen Itza, Mexico 43

Fig. 21 Left - Irene is standing at La Iglesia Temple decorated with elaborated masks of Chaac, the Rain God. 44

Fig. 22 Right – One of the serpent heads at the base of the pyramid stairs at Chichen-Itza, Mexico. 44

AWAKENING LOVE'S VIBRATIONS

Fig. 23 Palenque Ruins - Temple of the Foliated Cross is the small one in the middle, with triangular openings above the doorway and windows above the first level. The temple that appeared in my dream. 46

Fig. 24 Another view of temples at Palenque. 47

Fig. 25 Irene is standing in front of Siqueiros's mural. 48

Fig. 26 Robert, Irene, Donna, and Don are loving a big tree. 56

Fig. 27 Irene Vincent, *Shaman Dream Dance*, 1984, monotype: oil on archival black paper, 24"H x 24"W. 58

Fig. 28 Irene Vincent, *Cosmic Dance*, 1984, monotype: oil on archival black paper, 30"H x 30"W 59

Fig. 29 I. Vincent, *Medicine Woman Speaks*, 1985, monotype: oil on archival paper, 24"H x 18"W 60

Fig. 30 Irene Vincent, *Echoes of Devotion*, 1985, monotype: oil on archival paper, 24"H x 18"W 61

Fig. 31 Irene Vincent, *Some Enchanted Meeting*, 1985, monotype: oil on archival paper, 18"H x 24"W 62

Fig. 32 Irene Vincent, *Butterfly Woman*, 1985, monotype: oil on archival paper 18"H x 24"W 63

Fig. 33 Irene Vincent, *Inner Spaces*, 1985, monotype: oil on archival paper (ghost print) Sold 63

Fig. 34 Irene Vincent, *Shamanic Journey – Transmutation*, 1984, monotype: oil on archival paper, 18H" x 24W" 64

Fig. 35 Irene Vincent, *The Kiss*, 1985, monotype: oil on archival paper, 18"H x 18"H 64

Fig. 36 Irene Vincent, *Bird Man Meets Cat Woman*, 1985, monotype: oil on archival paper, 24"H x18"W 66

Fig. 37 Irene Vincent, Back view of *Molting of the Mermaid*, 1986, Acrylic painted over clay sculpture 69

Fig. 38 Irene Vincent, Side view of *Molting of the Mermaid*, 1986, sculpture, 14"H x 19"W x 28"L 69

Fig. 39 Julie, Irene, and Brenda are attending Irene's exhibit, Irvine Art center, 1986 70

Fig. 40 Left - I. Vincent, Sketch of *Missile Totem of the Ejecting Heart* 70

Fig. 41 Right - I. Vincent, Sketch of *The Universe and Misguided Missiles* 70

Fig. 42 Irene praying at Yogananda's Gardens in Encinitas, CA 72

Fig. 43 – Left - Guruji blesses Irene at Yogananda's Gardens in Encinitas, CA. 73

Fig. 44 – Right - Swami Vishnudevanand Saraswati of Allahabad, India at Kuma Mela Gathering. Photography by Carlos Ballantyne. 73

Fig. 45 Irene and Guruji are standing in the background. Sushil, Don Chase, and Shantanand are in the foreground. 74

Fig. 46 Irene Vincent, *Seeking Oneness*, 1986, acrylic on raw canvas, seven canvases bolted together, 12ft. H x 12ft. base. 76

Fig. 47 I. Vincent, quick study for *Seeking Oneness*, 1986, charcoal drawing on paper, 13"H x 8.5"W. 77

Fig. 48 I. Vincent, *Oneness in Thought*, 1986, acrylic, charcoal, and gesso on paper, 64"H x 24"W 78

Fig. 49 Irene is standing with *Seeking Oneness*, acrylic on raw stretched canvas. 79

Fig. 50. Jim, Robert and Irene are standing in front of the Golden Buddha in Thailand. 83

Fig. 51 Our tour group in Thailand 84

Fig. 52 Left - Elephant ride in Northern Thailand 84

Fig. 53 Right - View of the snake guardians and monks coming down the stairs. 84

Fig. 54 Left – Irene is standing near a Tibetan refugee village's gate. 85

Fig. 55 Right - Irene is in a Poppy field 85

Fig. 56 Irene is standing next to a snake guardian at the steps below the Tibetan temple....................86
Fig. 57, Fig. 58, & Fig. 59 Vincent, *Mayan Venus/Cat Goddess Singing to the Stars,* 1987, clay sculpture, 13.5"H x 8"W x6"L...89
Fig. 60, Fig. 61, and Fig. 62 I. Vincent, *Mayan-Spiral Venus,* 1987, clay sculpture, 10"H x 5"W x 5L" 90
Fig. 63, Fig. 64, Fig. 65, & Fig. 66 Irene Vincent, views of *Star Being,* 1987, clay sculpture, 9"H x 3.5"W x4.5"L...92
Fig. 67 Vastness of the ruins and jungle at Tikal, Guatemala. 96
Fig. 68 Irene reflecting upon the ancient pyramid stairs covered in overgrown roots. 96
Fig. 69 Irene and Robert are at the ruins in Tikal, Guatemala...97
Fig. 70 View of the Mayan pyramids at Tikal, Guatemala..97
Fig. 71 After the climb, Robert is relaxing and enjoying the view of Tikal. 98
Fig. 72 - Left - Colorful Guatemalan girls walking near Lake Atitlan. 98
Fig. 73 - Right - Colorful Guatemalan girls walking near Lake Atitlan 98
Fig. 74 I. Vincent, *Planetary Alignment for Dream Time,* 2003, 4'H x 3'W, oil paint over acrylic on canvas. 100
Fig. 75 Machu Picchu, Peru..105
Fig. 76 Irene hiking on Huayna Picchu. 106
Fig. 77.- Left - Nazca Lines, Peru – monkey image, view from the airplane. 108
Fig. 78 - Right - Astronaut image as seen from an airplane. 108
Fig. 79 Vincent, *The Cat's Dream Comes True,* started a few years after the dream in 1989, 60"H x 47 ½"W, Repainted 2007, oil over acrylic and sand on canvas. 114
Fig. 80 Irene, Swami Sahajananda, and Robert sailing in Newport Harbor, CA 140
Fig. 81 The geometry of the ancient buildings at Mitla 147
Fig. 82 Tule Tree 147
Fig. 83 Stele of dancing figures at Monte Alban 147
Fig. 84 Irene and Vera at Monte Alban, Mexico...148
Fig. 85 Stele of creation image at Monte Alban,Mexico 148
Fig. 86 Irene and Vera are standing on top of the Temple of Inscriptions, Palenque, Mexico. 154
Fig. 87 Pakal's tomb, Palenque 155
Fig. 88 Crossing the log bridge to Bonampak, Mexico...155
Fig. 89 Irene stuck in the mud on the way to Bonampak ruins...155
Fig. 90 Irene drenched up in the doorway of the pyramid in Bonampak 156
Fig. 91 Stele of slave taken prisoner at Bonampak 156
Fig. 92 Irene Vincent, *Spirit Bird & Snake Singing to the Stars,* 60"H x 40"W 160
Fig. 93 Irene Vincent, Photo by Jesi Silveria 163

AWAKENING LOVE'S VIBRATIONS

Fig. 1 In 1984, Irene is posing in front of *Journey of the Soul*. 1984, acrylic paint, cheese cloth, and paper on raw canvas, 65"H x 92 ½"W

Introduction

*I*F YOU ARE IN SEARCH OF INNER MEANING and are interested in knowing the spiritual transformative power of symbolism to enhance your life through art, dreams, and visions, then you will enjoy reading *Awakening Love's Vibrations*. If you are in search of the ultimate cure to understanding your relationships, *Awakening Love's Vibrations* will help to expand your perceptions of love.

During this journey, I felt universal love in many forms and ways. I felt love as a vibration, as a wave, as a wholeness and as a oneness. I experienced love as emotion, thought, and feeling coming from the heart-mind that creates all existence, which at the same time is deep silence, deep peace, and an all-embracing nothingness. This universal love lies in our DNA waiting to be activated, or perhaps it's always activated, but only veiled.

At age 32, I was a romantic idealist at a crossroad, balancing both art and my business, disappointed with worldly love and saddened that my political art might not succeed in bringing peace to the world.

Two things happened that quickened the next seven years. I had been making political art, hoping to raise the consciousness of people, but after realizing that trying to shock people into consciousness by showing them the problems of life, it didn't necessarily encourage them to find the solutions.

When I changed my question from what are the problems of life to what are the solutions for the problems, the essence of the question became, "What is love, a love beyond family, beyond tribe, and our culture? What is a universal love beyond sentimentality?"

This question helped create my painting, *Journey of the Soul* which then inspired me to make a commitment to my soul's journey. Once I made the commitment to my soul's journey and to discover what is *universal love*, doors of perception opened and teachers appeared.

The desire to know a greater love drew yogis into my life. I saw them as Olympic stars in their own right. These spiritual teachers were people with an untiring dedication and discipline to know their souls, their higher spiritual selves, and to become ultimate vessels of love. After experiencing waves of bliss emanating from Swami Sivananda Radha, Swami Sahajananda, and Swami Vishnudevanand; I wanted to know so much more, hooking me on my quest for wisdom. I do my best to represent and share the wisdom and insights of my teachers.

In my memoir, as I learned to decipher the meaning of symbols that appeared in my art, dreams and visions, these symbols became a language to my soul. Dreams guided me to travel to ancient Mayan ruins. Dreamtime intertwined with my daytime reality, healing me of a deadly flu, healing me of grief over my cat's death, and guiding me to be initiated by the Dalai Lama. I found when I asked the cosmic universe for help, especially when it was for my soul's greater good and the greater good of all, it brought solutions.

My quest to know my soul's purpose drew like-minded people and esoteric teachers into my life, people on a quest to find their true selves. Soon, I was no longer alone and developed a supportive community. As my creativity and clarity of mind blossomed, my jewelry business's success brought me financial independence. This in turn supported my spiritual adventures.

By working with my sculptures and paintings in a similar way as with dreams, my art became a consciousness-raising process and my channeling of visions became more pronounced. And as I explored hatha yoga, tai chi, shamanic drum journeying and other esoteric arts, each helped to transform my mind, body, and spirit, bringing in new experiences and synchronicities. Each art form gave me a deeper understanding of life.

Traveling to ancient sites made me even more aware of universal symbolism and helped me to honor the sacredness contained in all ancient cultures, a connection to our soul's humanity. Also, I became sensitive to the energy radiating from ancient sacred sites, the different vibrations and frequencies aligning and attuning my body to the Earth's healing resonance.

What I experienced is that this *cosmic love feeling* brings joy, bliss, peace, creativity, and a clarity of mind to exist well on this earth plane, and to be of benefit to all sentient beings. So, I wish to share my story, *Awakening Love's Vibrations* and hope that from vicariously experiencing my different explorations, you will be inspired to keep seeking and igniting your heart vibrations of universal love, joy and bliss.

CHAPTER ONE

Pushing Back the Illusions of Darkness

*F*EAR AND DOUBT RUSHED over me as I stared down at my freshly mixed pile of wet plaster, and then glancing back at the nude male model. I thought, *How in the world am I ever going to get this pile of mushy plaster to turn into something resembling a human figure?* Reaching for the bottom of my tee shirt, shaking it, I pulled it away from my sweaty chest, feeling the cool air rush up it. *Oh God, what did I get myself into? I'm a painter, not a sculptor. I could come up with some story and get out of here. Be brave, Irene. After all, most new situations in life seem to need an essence of bravery.*

Even so, the model posing on the platform with his glistening ebony skin and his anatomically beautiful butt, back and shoulders, was awe-inspiring. To me, though, the human form has an inherent beauty no matter whether fat, skinny, or otherwise. This beauty is about the human form's essence, being able to express emotion and energy coming from its soul. I only hoped to capture some of that essence on canvas and now in plaster.

Taking a deep breath, I began smearing the plaster over the wood, wire, and thistle rope base. The plaster readily stuck to the rope, allowing me to construct the model's form. After mixing plaster and water, I had only a fifteen-minute time frame before the mixture dried in order to get a layer on and form it. Then the dried plaster could be filed and chiseled. About every thirty minutes the professor rotated the model ever so slightly and we would rotate our sculpture to match the new view.

The sensuous cool feeling of the plaster caressing my fingers through the latex gloves sent erotic shivers through my body. Its fluidity allowed me to smear the plaster on the figure, making expressionistic marks and still give the form some anatomical structure. Joyful sensations and playfulness soon dissolved my fears.

With my imagination taking flight, I knew before the next day of modeling that my sculpture was going to be a Cat Man. A cat's head on my sculpture would symbolize him as being an independent freethinking person. Just doing a representational head of the model meant nothing to me. I needed to relate to it somehow.

Our group consisted of fifteen artists with our pedestals circling the model in the large, high-ceilinged, cement-floored room that always felt slightly cold. Most of us there had been making art of some kind for a number of years. After we had worked on our sculptures for six three-hour classes, only one artist declared her sculpture complete. I put my unfinished Cat Man into my car and began my drive back to my warehouse studio where I had moved to after my separation from Ron, who was still my business partner.

The studio was located across from the famous Angel Baseball Stadium in Anaheim, California. Toward the end of the complex were some train tracks and a strawberry field that attracted some healthy sized rodents. One, the size of a cat, had recently eaten through my office wall. We had had our show-down, whereupon he skidded to a halt as I screamed and jumped onto my dining table, a fork clunked against the cement floor, then a frozen silence prevailed. Our eyes pierced into each other's souls. Feeling a psychic transmission of some kind, I whispered firmly to him not to come back or I might have to kill him. I knew I didn't have it in my heart to hurt this creature so I prayed really hard for it not to come back. Even though I had stuck some wire scouring pads in the hole and plastered it closed, I often shivered while walking through the front office door, for fear of encountering the large rodent again. Not knowing how much longer I could bear living in this cold space, I wanted to complete as much artwork as possible.

When I arrived at my studio, I sat in my car wondering as to the best way to get this fifty-pound sculpture inside. I was a petite five foot one inch, hundred and seven-pound woman. I didn't want to wait until Robert, my new boyfriend got back from his college classes around 10:30 PM.

Anxious to work on Cat Man, I wheeled a small table out to the car. Staring at the sculpture, I took a deep breath, bent my legs, and struggled to get him on top of the worktable. Holding him with one hand, I used my other hand and legs to push the table into the main studio room. It was a wobbly venture, but we made it without incident.

Fixing myself a cup of coffee, I inhaled the fine Columbian aroma that now mingled with the dank air of the studio. Sitting in a chair, taking a sip of coffee, I stared at him. Thoughts and feelings welled up inside me about the existence of conflicts within myself and from life's experiences.

Jumping up from my chair, I began painting with liquid red paint on Cat Man's right side. Using a small brush, I pushed the paint into all the nooks and crannies of the textured surfaces, enjoying the patterns the paint created in flowing down the sculpture. Then I painted his left side a deep blue-black.

After painting him half deep blue-black and half red, I felt like it represented a split within my own being, that sense of separation I sometimes felt with life, with love, and with others. This felt ominous to me. Something had to be done quickly, but the paint needed to dry. A hair blower sped up the process.

Suddenly feeling irked, I thought about a previous art professor, Frank Dixon. He had once said that stopping your painting at a point where it agitates you is the surest way to keep the painting going, so that you finish it. There was some truth in that statement, although this was annoying me way too much to quit.

While imagining different colors for the final coat of paint on Cat Man, I remembered gold to be a magical alchemical color. Quickly, I mixed golden paint with water and medium, making it translucent. Next, I painted a golden outer layer, which brought the two underlying colors, representing dual energies, into a unity. By painting the golden outer layer semitransparent, I wanted to show that Cat Man saw through the illusion of the dualities and recognized that in reality there is only "one energy."

Fig. 2 Irene Vincent, sculpture, front side view on base - *Cat Man Pushing Back the Illusions of Darkness*, 1984, acrylic paint on carved plaster, mixed media, cheesecloth, wood etc., 71"H x 34"W x 30"L

Fig. 3 Irene Vincent, sculpture without pedestal, back side view - *Cat Man Pushing Back the Illusions of Darkness*, 1984, acrylic paint on carved plaster, mixed media, cheesecloth, wood etc.

Feeling relieved of my anxiety, I stood back and once again starred at the new golden Cat Man. He looked like he was pushing against images that appeared on the inside of his wooden frame, as though he were pushing back these illusions in an attempt to find the essence of truth. Thus, I called the sculpture, *Cat Man Pushing Back the Illusions of Darkness* (see Fig. 2).

Cat Man had an Egyptian look to me, so I designed him a pyramidal base in wood, which Robert happily put together for me. Using cheesecloth and medium, I formed horizontal textured lines on the bottom of the base. These lines symbolized the energy of the primordial soup, the beginning of creation.

When I thought of ancient Egypt, the sun god Ra came to my mind. First I glued more cheesecloth to the wooden base, forming rising energy lines depicting the sun's life giving energies. On the entire base, I painted thin layers of red for passion and a deep blue black to represent deep space. My thoughts were shifting to understand the yin and yang of life, and by giving my thoughts a crystallized material form it had helped me to experience these concepts more deeply. *Ah, such is the power of art.*

Glancing at my watch, I picked up the phone, thinking, *I hate checking in with Ron on my day off work. It really blows my sense of peace and creativity. I have to switch gears in my mind. Is this mirroring part of the duality that I'm trying to make whole in my art with the transparent layer of gold paint?* But there was a part of me that took pride in the fact that I could still manage the jewelry boutique with my ex-husband.

"Hi Ron, it's Irene. How were the jewelry sales today?"

"Jan sold a three-thousand-dollar diamond ring mount. We need you to make an appraisal for the customer's diamond tomorrow before we send it off to the repairman to set her stone."

"I'll get there a little early before anyone shows up. Otherwise the day may get too hectic. Anything else?"

"Yeah, Sheila and Vicki are fighting over a sale. Listen to their stories tomorrow, read to them the applicable parts of the policy book, and then let me know what you think. Then I'll make a decision on how to split the sale between them."

Sighing, I replied, "I wish they could learn to make these decisions on their own."

"Me, too. I wrote you a list of things to do. The main one is for you to get together a list of all the jewelry you need to buy in Los Angeles on your next day off."

"Remember, I have sculpture and figure drawing classes on Thursdays, I said. I'll have to go on Friday. I'll take the train because the traffic is dreadful on Fridays. I'll inventory jewelry on Saturday for at least three hours. Then I have stuff to do."

"I have to go. A group of customers just walked in and it's time to close down the store," Ron replied. "Talk with you tomorrow."

I sat there feeling drained. *I have to deal with the sales girls fighting tomorrow. If only I could have a real day off work, like they get. My real escape and happiness is when I'm working on my art. It gives my mind a focus, an escape from life's normal conflicts, giving me a sense of peace. There are challenges in creating art, but those don't affect me in the same way. I guess because the process becomes an adventure, giving me insights into my soul. Perhaps my emotions are involved differently. It's just my art and me. With people, I feel their anger, hurt, and hopelessness and I don't know how to maintain peace in the midst of it. If only I could see my "earning a living" life as an adventure, too.*

CHAPTER TWO

From Politics to Prayer: Missile Totem

AFTER AN EMOTIONALLY DRAINING day at work, it felt good to be alone in my Lincoln Continental, gliding my hands over the smooth wood part of the steering wheel and sinking down into the soft fabric seat. On the 405 freeway, fast drivers zoomed around and sudden stops jolted cars to a halt, but this was a time to switch gears from work problems to thoughts of art. During the forty-minute drive home from the jewelry store, creative ideas flowed on how to make a missile-totem sculpture.

I wanted to be through with making political art, to spend my time contemplating 'universal love.' However, almost every day my jewelry store was patronized by people who worked for the defense industry that built missiles. It seemed a large part of the southern California economy was based on weapons of mass destruction. My customers didn't want to think about their involvement, since it supported an upper middle class life style. It seemed they were sworn to some kind of secrecy. Plus, it was 1984, when so many the newspapers regularly surmised what areas might be annihilated if some rogue president or king hit a button.

Political images and visions came so easily to my mind because I was always thinking about the headlines and the problems of society. Since painting *Journey of the Soul* (see Fig. 1), I felt that images of love would be a greater solution for bringing people to awareness, rather than showing the problems in life. But with my mind caught in its old patterns, it was taking a conscious effort to enter this new realm of thinking.

One canvas, *Missiles and Coffee Cups,* (see Fig. 4) had both scared me and empowered me in the process of painting it. Missiles loomed in the sky ready to attack. It felt too real. I shook inside when I looked at the image, feeling like I was helping to create the possible disaster.

In contrast, the missiles were painted in luscious strokes of vivid color that enhanced the painting's aesthetic, which I visually enjoyed. However, after revisiting my sense of responsibility, I decided to paint over the missiles, blotting them out. I then painted a white border of missiles with the letter X painted over them, symbolically eliminating them.

In doing so, I felt empowered. In cave paintings, primitive men often painted beautiful images invoking a successful hunt. Other tribal artisans painted for healings and prayers. This image had conjured emotions in me similar to how indigenous cultures must have felt in painting some of their images. *Missiles and Coffee Cups* became a prayer of hope for me, a hope that mankind wouldn't annihilate itself. I felt a sudden heart-connection to shamans, who were spiritual healers who guided

AWAKENING LOVE'S VIBRATIONS

the spiritual well-being and health of their tribe. This transition piece had guided me to explore new esoteric vistas of life.

I had questioned my political art, how it reflected the problems more than the solutions of society. After contemplating the word 'solution,' I realized that the essence of ending conflict was 'Love.' This would have to be a powerful form of love, a love beyond sentimentality just for a family, a group, a tribe, a nation, or a planet; it was, indeed, a universal love. While contemplating the essence of love, I had painted, *Journey of the Soul* (see Fig. 1) sealing my desire and commitment to make my spiritual evolution a priority. So now, the key question to contemplate was, *What is universal cosmic love?*

Fig. 4 Irene Vincent, *Missiles and Coffee Cups,* Size: 50"H x 72"W, 1983
Acrylic paint is on unstretched raw canvas.
It rolls up in case you need to evacuate.

Pulling up to the warehouse door, I wondered, *Am I going to spend time and effort working on this huge sculpture I envisioned?* Robert's car was there, making me happy that he was home early. I ran into the studio. Sliding across the slippery concrete floor, unable to contain my laughter, I asked, "Robert, what are you up to?" Hammered up high on the wall were some work clothes with tools hanging in various directions forming an interesting composition.

"This is my contribution to modern art," he said, waving his arms and bowing, introducing it to some imaginary audience.

"Well, surely this piece would go for at least a million at auction," I replied.

Robert exclaimed, "At least!"

"Let's leave it hanging for a while. I rather like it," I said.

Robert had brought home some takeout food from our favorite Indian Restaurant. I happily set the plates and forks on our small round wooden table. Towels often covered the chairs to keep them paint-free from my soiled smudged clothes. The table overlooked the huge space filled with large paintings in progress. A multicolored hammock was the most comfortable place to relax.

Sitting in the chair, I filled my plate with Tandoori chicken, spinach with homemade cheese, and eggplant cooked with tomatoes and spices. Robert filled his plate.

Savoring a bite of the spinach, I said, "This food takes me to another place and realm. It's worth working just to be able to afford it."

Smiling, his mouth full, Robert managed, "Mmmm!"

"Robert," I said, "today I had a vision for a modern-day totem in plaster that would blend the inanimate and animate: missile shaped body, eagles' claws, and human heads. It would be about six foot high."

"That sounds interesting," he said.

"Yeah…but I feel I'm supposed to be having visions of *universal love*."

"It sounds like you're transforming the missile with human attributes and healing elements. I think you should build the missile totem," he replied.

"I figured out in my head the wooden structure part. If I draw a template on paper of the eagle's legs and claws, would you be able to cut that out of plywood for me?"

"Sure, I could get it done this weekend," he said.

"Okay then, a missile totem it is. Oh, I also need some kind of tube for the center to join the legs."

Robert said, "I'll help you rig something up. How are you going to get the plaster to stick?"

"I'll use a loose hemp thistle rope and wrap it around the whole piece. Plus, I suspect it'll be mighty heavy, so I'm going to build it on a square platform with wheels."

Fig. 5 Irene is posing while sculpting *Missile Totem* in her warehouse studio in 1984.

Fig. 6 Left - Irene is posing with *Missile Totem* in 1984.
Fig. 7 Right Irene is painting the first layer of red on *Missile Totem* in her warehouse studio.

All my spare moments were focused on *Missile Totem*. I loved the process of smearing on the wet plaster; it was so tactile and sensuous, and effortless to carve when it was still semi-wet. In carving it after it dried, I noticed I was breathing in too much dust. My throat was starting to swell. After that, I wore a mask.

Also, if I made a mistake, more plaster could be smeared over it. I had read that some great stone sculptors had to mix crumbled stone and wax to fill in their mistakes. Still I had no desire to chip away at stone, not with all the noise it generated.

After contemplating the powers and forces on earth behind the missiles, thoughts and images formed in my mind of how governments were out of balance. I used images of both the former U.S. President Ronald Reagan and the past Russian Leader Leonid Brezhnev to represent the over-masculine sides of power (too much logic). For the third world countries, I used a four-breasted masked image to represent the over-feminine side of power (too much emotion). This equated to humankind out of balance.

Between Reagan's ear and Brezhnev's ear runs a snake-like arrow to show stubborn miscommunication and non-trust. None of the countries' representatives have arms, a kind of pun on the arms' race. What would ordinarily be the missile's wings have metamorphosed into powerful-clawed eagle legs.

After finishing the basic carving, I smoothed the finished plaster piece with a fine grade of sand paper and then painted it with a layer of bright transparent red paint to represent blood and passion, giving the totem an essence of life. A layer of grayish transparent green muted some of the red areas and filled in other areas, adding contrast. The green symbolized the plants of the earth. A deep purple and blue with a hint of black painted between the legs represented deep space.

On one of the four sides of the missile I drew primitive men fighting each other with their spears. They fought "one on one" so they could still see into the eyes of their victims, unlike a nuclear conflict. Bows and guns furthered the distance to kill another human, rendering them more abstract to one another. Certain mathematical formulas and concepts of the universe, such as Einstein's Theory of Relativity helped develop these missiles. And as the abstract formulas evolved to develop the missiles, so did millions of possible victims become abstract mere statistics annihilated at the push of the button. To show this concept, I painted the transition from the primitive men to the mathematical formulas on one side of the totem.

As a ritualistic act of prayer, on one of Reagan's eagle legs I painted words such as *caring, compassion, kindness,* and *love*. I painted these same words in Russian on one of Brezhnev's legs.

To further transform this totem into a prayer for peace, I painted tantric symbols for the elements (earth, water, air, fire and ether) on the base, between each of the totem's four legs. We are all made of these elements.

At the top of the totem I painted small human figures holding hands and dancing around the missile's point, with the last figure holding up these elemental tantric symbols as a prayer. For me, *Missile Totem* (see Fig. 8) became an art piece that not only showed the problem, but also the inherent solution.

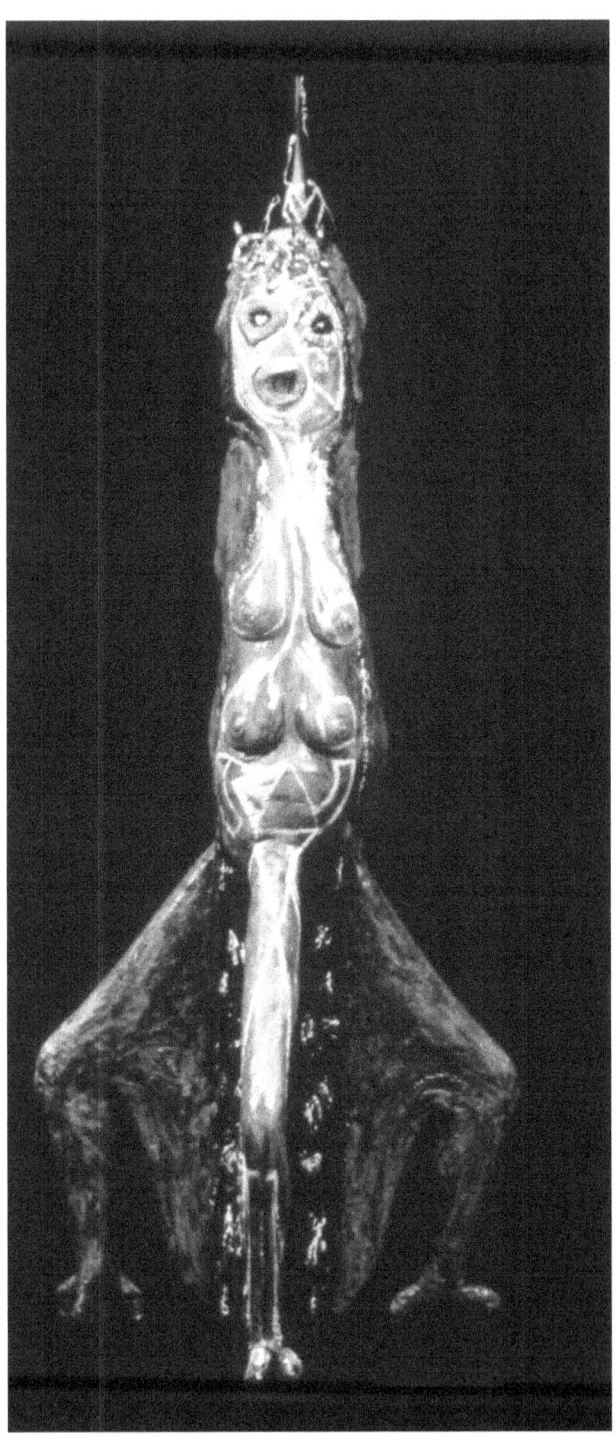

Fig. 8 Irene Vincent - The first view of three sides of *Missile Totem* is a four-breasted masked woman, which implies too many emotions, thus imbalance. She represents third world countries. 1984, 80"H x 24"W x 24"L. Acrylic is painted on carved plaster over a wood base.

Irene Vincent

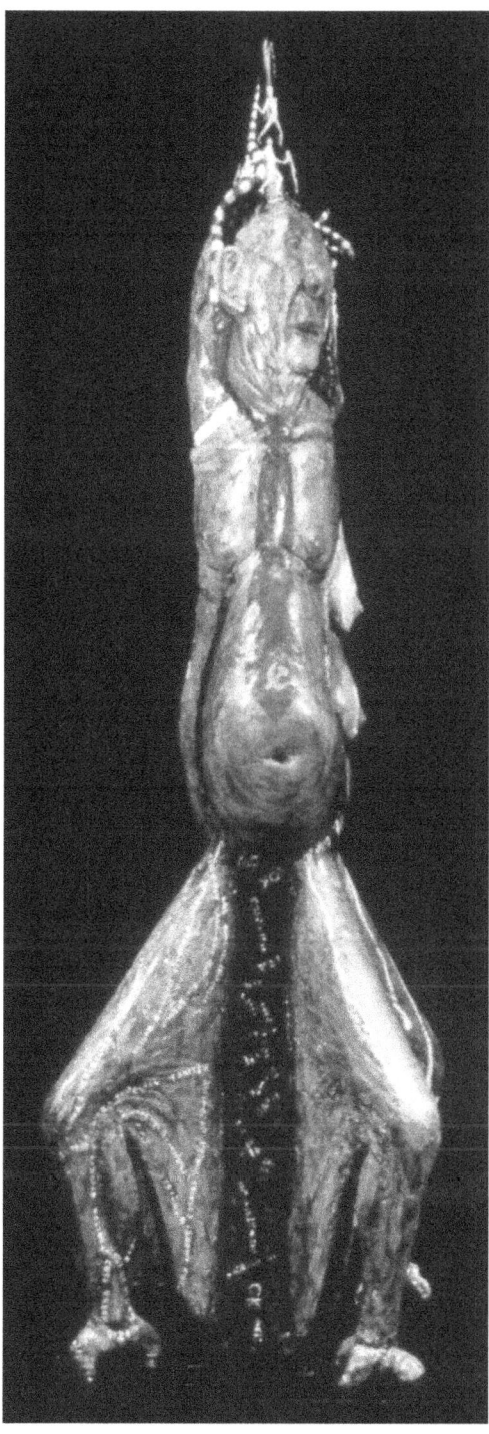

Fig. 9 – Irene Vincent - The second view of *Missile Totem* is an image of the former Soviet Leader, Leonid Brezhnev, representing Russia. It depicts that power ruled by too much logic and not enough heart is out of balance.

AWAKENING LOVE'S VIBRATIONS

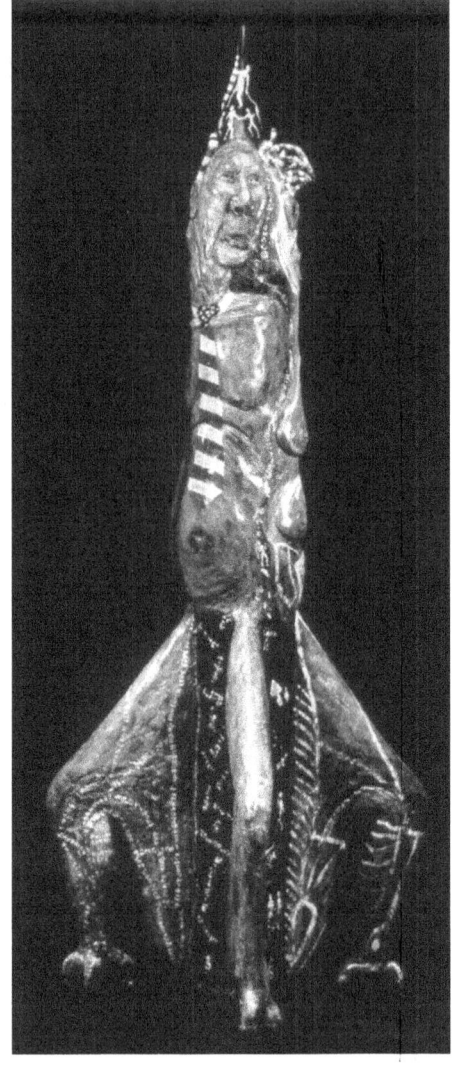

Fig. 10 Irene Vincent - The third view of *Missile Totem* is an image of the former United States President, Ronald Reagan, also meaning that power ruled by too much logic, not enough heart is out of balance.

As I was completing some of my larger pieces of art, I decided I really wanted out of the dismal cement environment of the warehouse. I missed looking out a kitchen window at green trees while I did the dishes, a precious moment of contemplation.

Because past landlords had forced me to pay for unused months, I had to muster up the courage to call the landlord.

I asked, "Bill, if I find a more suitable place to do my art, will you let me out of the lease?"

"Yes, Irene, I had received your message that the welders next door have been harassing you. They were actually thinking of renting your warehouse in addition to their own, which might be why they're acting that way toward you. As soon as you find a place to move to, just notify me and I'll draw up the paperwork."

"I'm deeply grateful," I said.

I started searching for a new place to live.

CHAPTER THREE

From the Ghetto to New Meadow

REACHING AN AGREEMENT, Robert and I decided that I wouldn't look for an apartment much farther south than Costa Mesa, if we were to continue living together. His drive north to Antioch University already took him more than forty minutes, which was about equal to my drive to work. If the apartment was close to the 405 freeway, then I could look a little more south, which I imagined would take us into better neighborhoods.

After searching the newspaper for an apartment, I made appointments to visit two of them in Costa Mesa. Driving up to the first one, I saw in the middle of the day a number of Mexican youths walking about the street and talking with neighbors. I wondered why they weren't in school. The apartment was small and old, musty with a hint of old grease, yet it cost much more than the warehouse.

My attempt to see the next Costa Mesa apartment was thwarted by sirens blaring from several police cars, orange tape cordoning off several neighborhood blocks, and a helicopter roaring and searching overhead. I was hoping to find my way out of there without incident.

I drove a bit farther north to Huntington Beach and Garden Grove where I knew the rents were affordable. Many of the apartment and housing complexes were older with high stucco walls, which hid the landscaping and trees behind the cities of cement. It felt ominous, so I gave up and drove back to the warehouse.

After telling my sculptor friend Dan what had happened, since he was the one who had suggested that I look in those areas, he now suggested that I look in Irvine, California. He told me that Irvine was known to be one of the safest, best planned communities in the US. It had trails, swimming pools, wide streets, luscious landscapes and even its own art center. He further enticed me by saying that the art center often featured Irvine-based artists.

After searching the newspapers, the thought of expensive rent for a tiny apartment with hardly a place to paint or a view was frustrating me, especially in contrast to the huge warehouse space. However, while driving around, seeing beautiful tree-lined streets and outdoor community swimming pools, I saw an intriguing sign: "Model Homes for Sale."

Thirty-five thousand dollars from my divorce settlement now sat in my bank account, but I had only a vague idea of what owning a house entailed. And that was my back-up money in case Ron and I sold the store next year. But then, if I used it up on rent, it would be gone anyway.

Suddenly I pulled the car over to the curb, mustering the courage to go into the intimidating model home's office door. Remembering the time Ron and I went to look at model homes, how the salespeople ignored us and didn't want to give us information, I sat frozen in my car seat. With my blouse sticking to my sweaty skin, I took in a soft breath and I imagined having a safe place to live, a garden, and a place to create huge paintings. Finally, I opened the car door and forced myself to walk through the scary door.

Pushing through the heavy wooden door, I stared down at a huge miniature model of little rectangles that symbolized the houses. It looked as if everything had been sold. My heart sunk. A tall man dressed in a suit approached me. His name was John and his gentle smile, kind eyes, and soft handshake, helped relieve me of my anxiety.

I said, "I'd like to buy a house, but I've no idea if it's possible. Do you even have one?"

In a genuine and soft voice John told me that I reminded him of his daughter. He explained financial details. Then with a whisper and a glint in his eye, he said, "There's possibly one last new home for sale in this builder's project, but it's in escrow for three more days. I've a feeling though that it'll be back on the market."

My eyebrows went up and a huge smile gleamed across my face. Smiling back, pausing for a moment, he said, "Before we talk any further, go and take a look at the house. Some men are working on it right now, so just walk in and let them know I've sent you. If you like it, come back and talk to me."

While driving to the house, I thought about the street number eleven, which meant in numerology "new beginnings" and New Meadow, the street name which depicted "green pastures or fields of flowers." Such thoughts uplifted me. But then I thought about being raised my first nine years in a Rochester, NY ghetto and that lingering fear of somehow ending up back there, the struggle to make it through college and then the struggles of running a business, all stirring old emotions that churned in the pit of my stomach.

Pulling the car over to the curb of this newly built home, a vivid memory came to me. Spontaneously, one Friday evening Ron had asked Scott, his best college buddy and Scott's girlfriend Alicia to join Ron and me for a trip to Disney Expo in Florida. Scott was one of the kindest people I'd ever met and I wasn't quite sure what he saw in Alicia. He was always trying to please her and support the notion of her being a Jewish princess, something in which she took pride. I didn't know what that meant until I met her.

Shortly after our first get-together with Scott and Alicia, I told Ron that she seemed to be trying to separate us. Ron confessed to me that during that same evening she had told him that he should make amends and stay true to his rich Jewish girlfriend in Baltimore. Why would he want to be with Irene who was struggling to work her way through college? Ron told me that he had already called his old girlfriend and broken up with her. He said he liked how we had fun and laughed so easily together.

But Scott was Ron's friend and off we were to Disney Expo. I'd always dreamed of going there as a little girl and now at 19 years of age, I was scared during our drive that something would happen and we wouldn't reach our destination.

During the drive, Alicia, who grew up wealthy, asked me what my dream house looked like. Suddenly embarrassed, I avoided telling her because I didn't even dare to dream about owning a house, because I didn't think it was possible for me to be a home owner. Skirting the issue, I asked her to describe her dream home.

"It's a large two-story Stucco home in Coral Gables," she said, "on the waterfront with a Yacht in the backyard and lots of luscious orange bougainvillea and exotic plants in the garden…lots of Palm trees circling the freeform swimming pool…oh, and a cabana."

I said, "Wow, your dream house sounds like Scott's dad's house. It sounds great. I want one just like it."

Jilted out of his conversation with Ron, Scott had chimed gently, "That might not be our first home, Alicia."

But I must say that her questioning me got me thinking about it as a real possibility. And now it was possible that same little girl had become financially independent and could own her own home. A waterfall of tears cascaded over my cheekbones, tears of letting go of all that past humility and pain. Shuddering like I had fallen into a frozen river, I blotted dry my face with tissue while checking in the sun visor mirror to make sure I wasn't covered in mascara. Composing myself, I noticed the single-story house with a huge dirt yard in which I could design a garden. The streets were wide with plenty of parking for friends. Getting out of the car, I headed to the front door of the house in Irvine.

Upon opening the door, I saw real tile floors, colored a sandy burnt sienna. I'd always wanted a home with real tiles, reaching down to tap them, making sure they were real. The closets all had mirrored doors. It was one story high with an atrium, so a garden with light could be planted in the heart of the home. The entry, living room, and garage had high ceilings, which meant that I could continue to paint large art. Peeking behind me to make sure no one was there, I put my arms in the air and danced in circles of joy.

I went back to John and told him I liked the house. Telling him my income, I asked, "Can you explain to me the finances needed?

"The house already has ten thousand dollars in improvements," John said, "and I'll give you ten thousand dollars more off the asking price, because the builder wants to move onto his next project. Give me a moment to figure out the financing."

After he calculated the financing, it looked as if I could afford the home. "Talk with your accountant and think about it for a few days," he said.

Three days later, John called me back. "I've good news for you, Irene. The house is available."

I asked, "How fast can I get a loan and move in?"

"As fast as the paper work can go through."

I was so excited that I even acted as a courier to move the paperwork around to whoever needed it. Within a month, Robert and I were moving into the house. I was thrilled about owning my first home. I knew I'd worked many hours to achieve it, yet I was so grateful to God. It was a relief to be out of the warehouse, a world of cement.

Ron gave me a small low interest loan for extra items.

I asked, "Ron, now tell me again, what is this for?"

"You're going to need curtains and other things that you haven't thought about. I want you to get your house together quickly, so you can concentrate on work." I was appreciative that Ron cared, but I also knew he was a workaholic. I was one, also, but my passion for art helped to create a balance in my life.

One night, while commuting home from work, I reminisced about meeting Robert at Donna's weekly art therapy workshop. Donna was an artist friend and a Jungian therapist. After a small group of us sat down on her couches and chairs, we relaxed while she read, guiding us through some magical world from which we would connect to our inner selves and emotions. Ribbons, papers, glue, buttons, strings, cardboard, crayons, paints, brushes, pencils, small found objects, and other colorful art materials were prearranged on a table. Choosing from these objects, we made an art piece that reflected our experience or how we felt that night. On finishing, we would share what our piece meant, as well as any insights we might have received. I'd always liked joining small groups to get to know people better. Now that it included art, it was even more fun.

Discovering that Robert liked going to art museums, intellectual movies, and was very social made him appealing. My planning with Donna to go see the movie, *My Dinner with Andre* went asunder because she went and saw it. Feeling bad, but having loved the movie, she suggested that Robert and I go see it together, which we did. After the movie, we went to a café for a late dinner, sipping and savoring our cappuccinos, talking the night away and sharing our life's aspirations.

Our next date was to go to the Los Angeles Museum of Art where we saw an Impressionist show. Then Robert agreed to go with me to another part of the museum to view some of my favorite paintings, discussing them as we went. I could feel his love and understanding for the arts, which was important to me.

We both liked sharing our dreams, exploring symbols, intuiting their meanings, and deciphering in a way that the dreamer is often symbolic of all the characters in the dream. Valuing my dreams as both a mirror and a guidance for my life, I was happy about the possibility of discussing them with my mate over breakfast.

Ron, a taskmaster, liked to keep us focused on work, expanding forward new projects. Although, Ron did become an extraordinarily fun person when we took trips, we mainly worked. Robert on the other hand liked to play and be social.

Robert had spent ten years in Canada at a spiritual ashram. His teacher, Swami Radha Sivananda had built and managed the ashram. She had told Robert that a couple should allow each other to grow spiritually, have time apart to take classes, then grow together. If individuals are self-fulfilled, they can give much more to the relationship. This concept gave me freedom to take classes without the stress of my mate wanting me home or at work all the time. Liberation bells rang loudly in my mind.

Being three years older than I, age thirty-five, Robert was handsome with fine facial features, medium-boned, an erect posture, endowed with a toned but lean muscular built formed from practicing ten years of hatha yoga. He stood five-foot eleven inches, easily taller next to my five-foot one-inch petite frame. He joked about his high intelligent forehead that had been created from his brown thinning hair.

After my divorce, I had moved into the warehouse. It had been scary for me to live alone in an industrial park. It was eerie and dark at night and there was no one to call out to for help. The vacated premises left me feeling vulnerable. Also, I realized I had been with a partner my whole young life, so companionship was very important. Dating wasted a lot of time, and since Robert and I had so much in common, it seemed only natural to be together.

We had just spent a romantic afternoon hiking to the Oak trees in Jasper's Wild Life Park. Rains had filled the dry riverbed, forcing us to take off our shoes. Slipping on moss, sliding over smooth stones, cool water caressing our feet, we forged our way across the rapidly flowing stream. Smells of sage and wild flowers wafted through the air. Upon reaching my favorite giant Oak tree the sun's rays streamed through the broad strong tree branches, warming our faces as Robert kissed my lips. We climbed up onto the huge embracing tree limb, nestling together while the humming, whizzing, and whirring of tiny insects harmonized, creating a symphony.

After a lovely dinner out, we had driven back to the warehouse. Yearning for cool drinks, I poured us two glasses of ice-cold orange juice. Sinking in the comfortable chairs near the small wooden dinner table, smiling at each other after a fun day, it was more difficult than I expected when I had asked Robert *the question*.

In a soft loving voice, I asked, "Robert, would you like to move in with me? We get along so well? I'm falling in love with you."

Shifting uneasily in his chair, Robert said, "I'm living at my mother's house and I don't have to pay her any rent." Pursing his lips, he continued. "Plus, I borrowed from her and I don't know when I'll be able to pay her back."

Tensing up, pain shot down my back. After hesitating, I went on, "I was hoping that you could help out," I said, "but I have to pay the rent anyway. How about I pay the rent and bills? Once in a while you can help me with lifting stuff or building my painting stretchers or something. Later on, when you graduate and get a job, then you can contribute to the household."

His posture stiffened and his back pressed hard into the cushion. "I'll have to work and pay my mom back before I contribute to you."

Acid filled my stomach, heading for my throat. I sighed. *Did I make a mistake? He isn't really saying that he wants to live with me. It seems to be negotiations.* I looked at him, choking back a tear that got stuck in my throat. I fell silent. Moments passed like days. Sadness drenched me in a dark veil, blotting out a beautiful day.

Robert stood up. "I'll think about it. My mom has become used to me living with her."

Standing up, twisting my lips, I said, "Are you going to live with her the rest of your life?"

With a gruff voice, he said, "I have to go home and study for an exam tomorrow. I'll let you know." He hugged me a quick goodbye.

After he walked out, tears rolled down my cheeks. I liked him, but maybe this was going to be too hard.

The next morning, he called me and said, "When should I move in?"

"Soon as you want to," I said, realizing I had just taken on a new responsibility. Even though he wanted to move in with me, some of the romance got lost in the way it happened.

We moved into my new house. In the front yard, we created a beautiful rock garden forming a riverbed with lush green ground cover and vibrant indigo flowers growing along the edges. Handpicked large elongated boulders were embedded vertically into the ground to create an ancient Stonehenge effect near the side door entrance. It was delightful to be able to look out a window and see our newly created garden of rocks and plants.

One morning when I walked outside, three little girls were sitting on the three wooden stairs at the front of the house. In a sweet melodic voice, one of the girls said she hoped I didn't mind that they were having a tea party, because they loved my garden. I told them that I was happy they chose my garden. A joy filled my heart. It wasn't just my garden; it was for the neighbors too.

In the atrium, we placed small boulders in the shaped of an infinity sign. The two largest boulders sat at each end, offering a surface to sit down. Colorful flowers and four leaf clovers filled the space around them, creating a magical spot.

The double car garage was transformed in an art studio. Workmen installed insulation on the exposed wooden framed walls and between the high ceiling beams along with a skylight, which let in natural light. On the left side of the garage, Robert built a wooden rack down from the ceiling as a place for me to store paintings. Special daylight spectrum lights were hung, accentuating the true colors of my paint.

No sooner had I thought about getting a cat when a half Siamese street cat snuck into my life. I tried to find his owner, but to no avail. Robert named him Samoa. After we fed him for three days and he got his strength back, he would growl and threaten to attack me if I didn't jump up to let him outside when he scratched at the door. Subsequently, I renamed him Fang.

We thought Fang needed a companion to help him calm down. Hence, we bought a sweet gray Persian cat named Purrsha. Life was once again peaceful. Or was it?

CHAPTER FOUR

Maps and Red Flags

WHILE WALKING DOWN the grocery store aisle, I remembered that during my first year with Ron, we had fought over what to eat at dinner. He only wanted hamburger or steak and hardly any vegetables, which was hard for me because I loved almost every vegetable. Over the years, and as we traveled, he added more and more foods to his diet. Robert and I didn't have that problem. However, some red flags were appearing.

After grocery shopping, I went back to the studio to have dinner alone. Robert had a late night at the university. I called my friend Donna who invited me to visit her. Donna always had a way of making me laugh, of lightening me up. Driving up to the curb near her house, I noticed how inviting her entry looked, with large green plants forming an archway just before an atrium leading to the front door. Everything beckoned *welcome*.

As I entered, Donna offered me hot tea and pointed to a deep green velvet covered chair near the matching couch. I sunk down into the chair with the cushions gently enveloping me. I felt at home; home in a heart sense, that I was wanted and loved.

After taking a sip of tea and sighing, Donna asked, "So, how are things going with you and Robert?"

Shaking my head, I asked, "Are relationships … always challenging? Robert seems to enjoy arguing."

She laughed, "You know, Don and I are always discovering something new about each other every day. It never ends. We used to fight about which way the toilet paper roll should be hung. We finally decided who ever hung it could put it on their own way."

"At least you came to a solution," I said. "Our latest fight was about maps on our way to Idyllwild. Before we left for the trip, he had the map spread out on the kitchen table and was looking at it for over two hours … on and off. I assumed he knew where we were going. He said that he would drive first. Once we were on our way, he handed me a map. I thought nothing about it. But then just before we were coming to where he thought we were to make a turn onto another freeway, he asked me which way to turn. I was shocked. I quickly opened the map and there weren't any yellow markings to show which way to turn. I always mark the map with a yellow liner. I grabbed a pen to mark where Idyllwild was and to figure out where we were. He yelled at me for putting a mark on the map. I got stressed out, but was able to tell him which way to go. I was in pain from all the tension by the time we arrived."

Donna asked, "Why didn't he want to mark the map?"

"He said he never puts marks on a map. I told him that when I plan a trip, I mark the map with a yellow highlighter, like Triple A does. Then I write directions on a sheet of paper, such as: right, north, and the cities I'm going towards as a list in big letters so I can see it while I'm driving. I told him I'll make a list route for any more day trips."

Donna said, "So did it resolve things?"

"I hope so. I had to figure the return route without putting any marks on the map. Other than that we had a pretty good time hiking in the mountains."

I continued, "Robert did mention that his spiritual teacher, Swami Radha, was coming to town soon. He told me that she offers a class on relationships up at her ashram in Canada. I wholeheartedly agreed that it would be wonderful to go visit her and take the workshop."

"Okay let's talk about art now," Donna said.

"Yes, let's do that!" I laughed, mocking myself for venting.

It was helpful to share our relationships, but it seemed that talking about art and movies was so much more fun.

CHAPTER FIVE

Swami Sivananda Radha: A Heart of Love

ON COMPLETING MY PAINTING, *Journey of the Soul* in 1984, I realized how much I valued the growth of my soul, my spiritual life. And as I read books on saints and monks, they magically appeared in my life. It was as if reading their stories fueled a deep longing within me to meet such enlightened people, thus bringing them into my life. Robert introduced me to his yogini teacher, Swami Sivananda Radha, who was one of these special teachers.

When she gave a spiritual lecture at his mother's house, I found her stories very inspiring. Her voice was soft, yet she spoke with an authority of self-actualized knowledge. Her voice and her being emanated love. A gentle breeze of joy, peace, and contentment washed over me as I listened to her stories. Never before had I felt that kind of love from anyone. I wanted to get to know Swami Radha.

I invited her to stay with Robert and me the next time she came to Southern California, offering to sponsor her lectures. A short time later, she came with a few of her disciples and stayed at my home. She gave a wonderful lecture and it was so uplifting for me to share my home.

She told me some of her inspiring life story. As reported in her book, *Radha: Dairy of a Woman's Search*, "she was born in Berlin, in 1911, into a liberal wealthy German family. In 1939, she was the first woman admitted to the Berlin School of Advertising. Radha's career was cut short by her opposition to the Nazis."

During her stay at my home, Swami Radha told me that her first husband, a German man with a kind heart, was killed while helping Jews escape out of Nazi-Germany. She remarried. Her second husband was a classical music composer and died shortly after they were married. She told me how she grieved for her deceased husbands and all the horror that had happened during World War II. After that, she immigrated to Canada, developing a career as a classical dancer.

Then she told me that, while meditating, she'd had a vision of her Guru, Swami Sivananda. He beckoned her to come and study with him at his ashram in Rishikesh, India. After corresponding with him through letters, she left everything behind her and went off to India for her powerful spiritual adventure. Under the guidance of Swami Sivananda, she met many evolved spiritual teachers. Soon after Swami Sivananda initiated Radha, he told her to go back to Canada and give spiritual guidance to people.

When she got back to Canada, she started giving lectures. She had been instructed to set up an ashram, but she could only hold faith it would occur. She told me how she was invited to work at a psychological institute to help heal the insane and imbalanced patients.

AWAKENING LOVE'S VIBRATIONS

Fig. 11 Irene, Swami Radha, and Robert are having breakfast at 11 New Meadow.

Fig. 12 Swami Radha visits.

Fig. 13 Swami Radha and I are in my backyard.

Even though she was helping the patients, it took a toll on her own health and balance. It was too draining. She recognized that once she had achieved a certain spiritual growth, it was better for her to work with people ready to meet her at her level of vibration and consciousness. As she put it, it's better for a person who has just overcome an addiction to help guide another addict.

She told me she was scared when she first started giving spiritual lectures, but as she spoke, words flowed through her. It was truly as if her guru was at her side, guiding her. Then, as her guru had predicted, disciples came to build a spiritual community, eventually constructing the ashram in Kootenay Bay, British Columbia, Canada.

Shortly after her visit, I took her three-day self-realization workshop called "Music and Consciousness" in San Francisco at a disciple's home, called a Shambhala House. I drove up the magnificent California coastline, with its high, winding tree-lined cliffs overlooking expansive vistas of blue purple waters turning into turquoises and greens, sparkling, setting the mood for inward contemplation. San Francisco's traffic threw me into a frazzle, however, so I booked a hotel room close by the Shambhala House.

The Shambhala House was a large three story Victorian style home. Many of the arriving students met first in the kitchen, sharing our excitement while making coffee and tea. Then we proceeded up a flight of stairs to a large room set up like a temple with pictures of yogis and holy people. A soft light flooded in through the large windows, casting serenity about the room. Thirteen comfortable chairs were arranged in a circle. Swami Radha walked in, beaming radiance and looking ever so elegant.

She explained to us the vibration power of the Mantra. When pronounced properly and chanted with sincerity, it would reveal its spiritual meaning and transform us. The sound and vibration of the mantra takes you to the source of the mind, which is spirit. Thoughts and worries fall away and the chanter becomes deeply relaxed and enters meditation. Sages originally intuited mantras while listening to nature and while in deep states of meditation. We chanted three OMs and then we sang some spiritually uplifting songs.

Lovingly, Swami Radha taught us to be responsible in our daily lives. As she spent time talking with each student and asking questions about his/her life, almost all of them blamed their parents for their present situation. The students ranged from twenty to fifty years old. After what seemed to me like endless questioning, they came to realize that they alone were responsible for the decisions that they had made for their lives.

"Once you take responsibility for your life," she said, "the quality of your life will improve." Some of her previous students explained how their individual self-questioning brought self-awareness that led to improvement of their mind, body and spirit.

When it came time for my interview, I said, "I already forgave my parents for whatever neglect I had blamed them for. At seventeen, when I set out on my own and realized how difficult it was to earn a living and work my way through college, I realized how much they sacrificed to take care of my siblings and me. They went through a lot of hardship to raise us. If anything, I take on responsibility too quickly."

She giggled and smiled at me, "Is that so? Tell me about your jewelry business and how you manage it?"

After listening to me, she suggested, "Write up the stories for the symbols used in the Native American Jewelry, the Hopi Kachinas, and the healing powers of the gem stones. That way, when a customer makes a purchase, the item will be extra meaningful to them. This may help increase your business."

"Yes, I've seen books on the power of gem stones and I have books on symbols. I'm sure I can talk my business partner into helping me write stories for the customers."

"Do you meditate?" Swami Radha asked.

"I think I do, but I haven't really been taught or trained."

"How do you get the visions for your art?" she asked.

I replied, "Sometimes I think about a word or a thought for years. During high school, I chose a word to contemplate each year. One year I chose the word *relationship*. I observed how people related to one another, how they mistreated each other and how they were kind to each other. It created a type of focus."

Continuing I said, "As I started to paint, I contemplated the meanings of such words as *transition of edge, subtleness, surface, depth, space* and *softness*. Then, as I became political, I would ask the questions: What is power? What is equality? What is fair? What is judgment? When I saw a problem in society, I'd sit at my dining room table surrounded with books on the subject. I'd read for a while, then just sit quietly and ponder the topic in my mind. Then out of the blue, when showering or walking, an image or vision for a painting would come."

Swami Radha said, "Some people say contemplation is a higher form of meditation. Irene, contemplate on *that: that which is most high*. Contemplate on *your higher self*. Contemplate on *spirit*."

I thanked her.

"Irene, do you have any questions before I move on to another student?"

"Yes, I have one more question," I said. "Swami Radha, how are you able to answer your students' endless questions in a workshop and still have so much energy? I'm drained by just observing this process of self-questioning. You're still glowing."

Everyone chuckled.

She said, "The answers channel through me, so they're not using my energy. My body is a divine instrument, for the divine energy to channel through, like music playing through a flute." She paused, showing a beautiful loving smile.

"Wow, that's something for me to contemplate," I said. "Okay, I'm finished."

For the next few years, Swami Radha stayed overnight and gave lectures in my home whenever she was in the area. One of her lectures was titled "Suspending Your Beliefs".

During her lecture, one person questioned, "If I follow what you teach, how do I know that I'm not being brainwashed or hypnotized?"

She answered, "Everything surrounding you is having an effect upon you. You're already hypnotized. Suspend your beliefs. Don't automatically believe anything I say or anything someone else claims to be true. Practice discrimination. For instance, suppose you practice a mantra. Observe your life and if it improves in quality, keep up your practice. If you practice yoga and your health improves and bad habits naturally diminish, you may want to continue practicing yoga."

Swami Radha gave another lecture titled "Identity".

She asked, "With what do we identify ourselves? Do we over-identify with our job, our family and our beliefs? Do we identify with our personality?"

She continued, "It's best to identify with *our higher self, our spirit*. That way our perception is that we are all one, helping us to make heartfelt choices."

She taught us to say "Namaste" to each other with our hands in prayer position at our hearts and to think in that moment, "May the divine in me salute the divine in you."

Saying "Namaste" as a greeting brought a joyful feeling to my heart.

Swami Radha taught us about different aspects of male/female relationships. She said that we needed to be whole within ourselves in order to be in a quality relationship. We needed to be aware of our needs and how to fulfill them within ourselves, rather than wanting or hoping that someone else will fulfill our needs.

I asked, "Shouldn't my partner make me feel complete?"

With a stern voice, she replied, "No, you need to be complete within yourself in order to have a fulfilling relationship."

Softening again, she said, "Make the growth of your spirit a priority and honor the growth of your partner's spirit. Give each other freedom and support to seek growth of spirit."

Then I asked, "What about the law of attraction? If I'm attracted to a man, does that mean he's my soul mate?"

Swami Radha replied, "Attraction and repulsion are no different from one another. You may be repulsed by first sight of a person, and he may be good for you in some way. And you may be attracted to a person and he may be harmful to you. Always take time to discriminate about who you want to spend your time with in life. Of course, the more you reflect upon yourself as spirit, the more you'll see clearly and be able to trust your intuition. Intuition is deeper than a surface attraction or repulsion."

She continued, "Furthermore, young people these days are quick to jump in bed with a partner. If you take at least three months to get to know someone, you'll discover if you'll want to really be a partner with this person. At my ashram, the notion of "free love" circulated around and a number of single students jumped in bed with each other. I gave a lecture and told them they were creating a Karmic bond when they have sexual intercourse with another person. It's very likely that they'll have to come back in another lifetime and marry that sexual partner. The students laughed! But then they looked at each other, and I could see that they couldn't imagine a full week with that person, let alone a lifetime. It was amazing that when the students contemplated that thought, free love and promiscuity at the Ashram ended."

One morning after one of Swami Radha's visits, Swami Radha and I were having breakfast at a table in my back yard on our wooden deck. It was a small yard but quite serene. Three high stucco walls enclosed the perimeter. Extending two feet out from these walls, natural cobblestones formed two-foot high raised planters. Orange and rose-colored bougainvillea plants flourished along with pink-yellow colored roses. A peach scent wafted through the air. Tiny vibrant purple and indigo-colored flowers accented the larger plants.

We were still in our pajamas, when Robert peeking from the window and looking rather mischievous, ran out to take our picture.

A bit upset, I said, "Robert, don't take our picture like this. We aren't dressed properly."

To my surprise, Swami Radha said, "Take our picture, Robert. This picture will show that I stayed overnight at Irene's house. She'll be able to put it in her book."

I stood next to Swami Radha wrapping my arm around her for the pose.

After Robert took a few pictures, I asked, "Swami Radha, what do you mean about a book? What could I possibly write about?"

"Irene, you managed to get yourself out of the ghetto, out of poverty, go to college, start a business, buy a house, and accomplish a degree of financial independence. And you make time to pursue your passion as an artist. You're only thirty-two years old. You can be an inspiration to other women. I have artistic students who don't take care of themselves. Perhaps you'll help them see the benefits of pursuing a balance in their lives."

"But, I didn't do this on my own. Other people inspired and helped me."

"Write your story and include how others helped you. Irene, I like to help my students obtain financial success as they gain their spiritual awareness. It makes it easier for them to help more people."

"I'll give this some thought," I said.

Swami Radha said, "Also, besides yoga, I suggest that women take up weight lifting. It helps them to keep their bones strong and to compete in a man's world."

"That's interesting. My business partner Ron trades with a gym owner for personal training. Perhaps, I could do that."

Robert ate his breakfast and disappeared from the table. He was true to his Gemini sign. He was either working with his hands fixing or making something, or doing research on his computer.

Suddenly, Swami Radha looked sternly at me and asked, "Irene you've had a number of partners in your life. What does the act of sex do for you?"

Surprised by her question and tone, straightening in my chair, and then leaning towards her, I whispered, "When I have sex with a man, I feel as if we become one, a type of merging. I feel that it's the closest to God that I can get."

"You know," she said, a soft intrigue vibrating in her voice, "there is no greater orgasm than the union of your spirit with cosmic consciousness. It's the ultimate orgasm. Your body is filled with a bliss and peace that no earthly orgasm will give to you." She smiled at me, got up and headed into the house.

I sat there quietly. *Wow, that wasn't expected. Is it because I'm sexually active that Swami Radha came up with this "ultimate orgasm concept"? Hmm, what would this ultimate orgasm feel like? The universe is a mystery. I know that a lot of people seek an ultimate high through drugs or sex. Sometimes they have visions, but their egos are involved, power struggles remain, and they don't gain a true bliss or peace. I love talking to the Divine Universe and would like to know it more intimately while in this human body. I had figured this event called "Enlightenment" was for a chosen few. Is "Enlightenment" even a possibility for me in this lifetime? I wonder what images of art might appear from these new contemplations?*

CHAPTER SIX

The Healing Power of "The Divine Light Invocation"

A LECTURE HAD BEEN PLANNED for later that day. Not knowing how many people would show up, I set up several chairs in the living room. Then the room was decorated with a few shimmering crystal vases filled with orange-yellow roses, garnished with green ferns, and interspersed with tiny white lacey flowers. Another vase was filled with fresh jasmine from my yard, emanating its euphoric essence into the air. Candles glowed in different areas around the room.

Soon, the room was filled with about twenty people. Just before Swami Radha began to speak, I lit some Patchouli incense, sending out scents of an earthy aroma with a fresh fruit smell. Swami Radha, always elegantly dressed, walked into the room, her presence causing a silence. We chanted three OMs bringing a deeper calm and silence to the room. As she spoke the love from her voice combined with the deeper truths of her words, transporting me to a space of cosmic inspiration.

Towards the end of her lecture, Swami Radha told us part of her life's story as she had explained in one of her many books, *The Divine Light Invocation*. She said that through sincere practice of this invocation one would gain a greater understanding of one's own divine nature. She told us about how she received her initiation into the ancient order of the *sanyasa* from Swami Sivananda on February 2, 1956 at the base of the Himalayas. And how, later that same day, she had wandered off to a nearby, cave-like ruin to meditate on what her new life looked like. She had a vision of the ancient Babaji, who taught her the Divine Light Invocation.

She explained that it's important for the devotee to be relaxed, receptive, and in the proper stance. It's important to develop your imagination and ability to visualize the light. She then related some of her personal stories of healing that had occurred for those that were blessed.

Glancing towards the window, I could see that it was twilight outside, that special time between day and night when silence imbues the air. I looked around at the images of powerful serene yogis newly adorning my walls; smiling faces radiating bliss, inviting one to another realm. Spiraling plumes of smoke off the tip of an incense stick drew my attention.

At that moment, Swami Radha said, "Let's all stand in a circle and experience the ancient invocation."

As everyone formed a circle, she peered over at Robert saying, " Would you please guide us through the invocation?"

Robert looked around at the individuals in the circle and said, "Begin purifying yourself in the following way. While breathing in, raise your arms above your head. Tense your body and hold your breath while saying: *I am created by Divine Light, I am sustained by Divine Light, I am protected by Divine Light, I am surrounded by Divine Light and I am ever growing into Divine Light.* Now visualize a beautiful lotus blossom at the crown of your head, opening to a shower of Divine Light coming down from the Heavens, flowing down through the crown of your head, filling your entire body with this divine healing energy. Then drop your hands to your sides with your palms facing outward, while exhaling… breathing and relaxing."

Continuing, in a gentle, harmonic tone, Robert said, "Once again, tense your body and inhale, but with your arms at your sides, palms facing out, holding your breath while mentally repeating: *I am created by Divine Light, I am sustained by Divine Light, I am protected by Divine Light, I am surrounded by Divine Light and I am ever growing into Divine Light.* Gently exhale and relax. Then concentrate on feeling a warm glowing light permeating your entire body, outside as well as inside. Visualize the Divine Light filling every cell, healing every cell, and illuminating every level of consciousness within the cells of your body. Feel every atom of your being merging with the light."

Pausing for a few moments, then continuing, he said, "Imagine the form of yourself standing in front of you, inside this circle. Visualize your heart chakra opening with the stream of Divine Light pouring out and extending to the feet of your imagined form, the light spiraling upward clockwise around your form and lifting your form up into the sky. See yourself merging with the source of the Divine Light above.

"Now choose someone to bless, usually starting with your parents, or the spirits of your parents if they have passed on. Imagine the outline of this person projected and standing in front of you. Feel your heart chakra opening with the stream of Divine Light pouring out, extending to the feet of the imagined human form, the light spiraling upward and clockwise around the form, lifting this being up into the sky. Visualize these people one at a time, merging with the source of the Divine Light."

Guiding us, he said, "I'm giving you a few moments to bless others, individuals and groups of friends, as well as projects in the same manner. Anytime your mind strays, go back to tensing, repeating the Mantra, and relaxing to keep your concentration."

It seemed as if time had stopped. My body felt more and more relaxed, filling with a sweet energy, which I figured to be bliss, something that people seemed to be seeking. A joy emerged as I was blessing people.

Robert's voice filtered through the deep silence, he said, "If anyone wants to say a name of a loved one or someone who needs a healing, you can say their name out loud and we can all visualize their form, a human figure, standing in the center of the circle and once again … feel your heart chakra opening with the stream of Divine Light pouring out, extending to the feet of the imagined human form, the light spiraling upward and clockwise around the human shape, lifting this being up into the sky."

People called out names and we each blessed the human forms, as best we could, in the prescribed manner. Minutes passed, silence reigned.

Robert's voice sung out, "Gently feel the presence of your body, breathe and relax, open your eyes, gaze upon the individuals in the circle, put your hands in prayer position, and say 'Namaste,' while thinking, 'May the divine in me salute the divine in you,' Give thanks and gratitude."

After a short while, Robert looked at Swami Radha. Smiling, she announced, "There is plenty of food and treats in the kitchen to partake of. Let's eat, while maintaining our peacefulness."

That evening, everyone left the house with a happy, peaceful face.

Soon after this first experience, I would beg Robert to guide me through the invocation. Each time I felt this gentle surge of loving energy flow through me. I was seeing the correlation between blessing others and how instantaneously the universe blessed us.

Over time, different experiences with my personal invocation practice guided me into making it more intricate. For instance, shortly after I had begun practicing it, I walked into a desert area near my friends' home in Albuquerque, New Mexico. It was an hour before sunset, but still an extremely hot day — the high nineties. In fact, I hadn't thought of bringing water with me, but I did remember to bring cornmeal and tobacco to sprinkle on mother earth before journeying on the path, a Native American ritual. Following a sandy path up a steep incline, some large colorful boulders enticed me to keep climbing. I chanted Om Mani Padme Hum, over and over, often combining different ancient traditions, honoring all that is sacred.

Of course, my imagination was saying, 'Please don't let me run into a snake or a mountain lion.' It always seemed that I saw snakes and scorpions on my hikes. That I shouldn't be alone was a thought, flittering like a firefly. Okay, Irene, I told myself, drop the fear.

After checking for critters, I snuggled up to an inviting boulder where I had a view of the path below. The clear blue sky seemed vast like the ocean, the vista expanding at least two hundred miles. I relaxed into the rock's curved shape. Practicing the Divine Light Invocation, I began blessing family, teachers, friends, and all the peoples on earth, but then I proceeded to bless all the angels, archangels, gods and goddesses, and the Supreme Universal Being.

Suddenly, I got scared. *Who am I to bless beings greater than myself?* I thought. In that same moment, an overpowering wave of energy came from the sky into my heart. I realized all beings are grateful to be blessed, all of us are this inherent love essence, and blessing another invokes the gentle vibration of love. Sitting there, imbued with bliss, I meditated for a while.

Carefully, I stepped down the steep, sandy stone-scattered path, slipping here and there, thinking about my new lesson. I made my way back to Don and Donnas' house where Donna had prepared a delicious meal. Still processing the day's events, I wasn't ready to share them yet, when Donna asked, "So how was your walk?"

I just replied, "It was hot, but very peaceful."

Don jumped into the conversation to talk about his new art students and the new poetry group that he had formed. Don and Donna had a lot of love in their hearts, but I wasn't always sure how they might receive any of my deeper spiritual experiences. So that part of myself I often kept quiet about, and there was a spiritual loneliness in that.

My personal use of the Divine Light Invocation became more intricate over time. The whole beginning part remained the same in invoking the light and purifying the self. Then I came to visualize my hand chakras (centers of my palms), opening with the healing Divine Light energy pouring out through them. Next I saw my heart chakra opening with the stream of Divine Light pouring out, extending to the feet of the imagined form of a person, first the self, the light spiraling upward clockwise around the form and lifting this being up into the sky, merging with the source of the Divine Light.

In sequence, I visualized the spirits of past, present and even future spiritual teachers. Then I blessed my parents and the spirits of deceased loved ones, then immediate family members, extended family, friends, acquaintances, and anyone who needed healing. I imagined the Divine Light spreading out over the neighborhood, blessing all my neighbors, then spreading out farther over the whole Earth, blessing all its peoples.

Then I put my pets and those of friends into the light as well, with the light spiraling around them and lifting them to the source. The Divine Light blessed all the animals of the world, those of water, earth and sky.

Next, I visualized the Divine Light blessing all the plants of the earth, water, and sky, and then all the elements: earth, water, air, fire and ether.

I visualized the Divine Light spiraling around the earth and the earth floating in the light. I invoked the Divine Light, blessing all the angels, archangels, gods, and goddesses. Continuing, I imagined the Divine Light overflowing from my heart, blessing all the stars and planets, all the universes and all the beings in all the universes.

I visualized the Divine Light spreading out over the far reaches of the universe, blessing That which is The Supreme Universal Being, That which is Most High, That which is My Innermost Indwelling Spirit, so within, so without, so without, so within, OM Tat Sat, So Be It, Om Shanti, Shanti, Shanti, Om Peace, Peace, Peace. I placed my hands together in prayer position. If I was in a group circle, I ended with the guidance of looking into each other's eyes and saying "Namaste" (May the Divine in me bless the Divine in you).

After much practice, I have found invoking the Divine Light to be an effective form of long distance healing and blessing. Anytime a loved one is sick, I place them in the Divine Light. If I hear someone say they are sick or their loved one is sick, I ask permission to put them into the Divine Light.

I trust that the Divine Universe knows what is best for a person's soul, believing that Divine Grace is always present and is present for the growth of our soul. Any request pertaining to the well-being of our soul as well as for those we pray for is immediately answered. Swami Radha's book *The Divine Light Invocation* has been an inspiration to reread and great for reviewing accuracy of the practice.

Anytime that I had doubts about this practice, God, Divine Mother, The Cosmic Universe gave me a sign to know I was on the right path. Also, I found an unexpected benefit: as I invoked the light and blessed others, waves of bliss filled me with a deep peace.

With these new practices, sweet synchronicities started to occur in my life. On my birthday, Robert and I went out to dinner. It was a forty-minute wait to be seated in the restaurant. We walked down the street in Newport Beach and came across an antique auction house that was holding a live auction in two hours. While browsing around the store, I saw a beautiful bronze statue of the Tibetan Goddess Tara. She was a healing Goddess. She was sitting upon a lotus in a meditating posture, with the sole of her foot facing up towards the heavens, her other foot facing down and resting on a lotus, symbolizing that she is rooted in Cosmic Consciousness and is always ready to help another being. Her right-hand gesture warded off things not conducive for the higher self. Her left hand held a lotus depicting that although the lotus grows in the mud, Tara is unaffected by the muck of the world.

As I melted into the statue's symbolic beauty, my heart opened, emanating love. *This would be a meaningful birthday present*, I thought. Some other people were admiring the statue. I walked over alongside one woman, telling her how much the statue meant to me. She told me that she also found the statue interesting. Three of us cast a bid for it. Then Robert and I went to dinner.

In returning to the auction house, we watched another lady make a bid higher on Tara. She noticed my sad face, however, and with a gesture of kindness she let my next bid be final.

The auctioneer said, "Sold."

I was grateful. For me, the statue of Tara symbolized being present for others and keeping an open heart and that was my soul's aspiration.

The next time I saw Swami Radha, she said, "Irene, I want to give you a mantra to contemplate and practice. Would you like that?"

"Of course," I said, my heartbeat leaping around from this feeling of being accepted into a new level, or realm.

"I want to give you the Tara Mantra," she said. "Do you know what she looks like?"

"Yes, I just bought a statue of Tara."

Swami said, "The words to the Green Tara's mantra are: Om Tare Tuttare Ture Svaha / Om Tare Tuttare Ture Svaha. Repeat Tara's mantra, visualize her image in your heart, and let her essence guide you."

Tears of joy flowed down my face. This initiation was so appropriate; Swami Radha hadn't known that I'd been contemplating the meaning of my new statue of Green Tara.

Fig. 14 Swami Radha

AWAKENING LOVE'S VIBRATIONS

Fig. 15 Don Gamble, Irene Vincent, Swami Radha, and Terrence Buie at the Ritz Carlton in Dana Point, CA

CHAPTER SEVEN

Trip to Swami Radha's Ashram

ONE MORNING WHILE we were eating breakfast, Robert suggested we go visit Swami Radha in Kootenay Bay, British Columbia. "Irene," he said. "I want you to see where I've lived for ten years. They're offering a weekend relationship course next month. We could improve our relationship."

"Okay, I could probably get five days off work. Let me ask Ron."

A month later, we flew to Calgary, then to Trail Airport and then took a bus to Nelson. Robert wanted to stay overnight in Nelson so he could introduce me to Mrs. Johnson, an elderly lady who had held Saturday painting classes for beginners. Robert gave her a phone call and we were on our way for a visit. As we walked to her home, I admired the town, surrounded as it was by a lake placed in the Selkirk Mountains. With childish excitement, Robert pointed out her home on the edge of the lake, "There it is!"

Upon arrival, Mrs. Johnson, a widow, graciously invited us into her small home. She gave Robert a big hug. "I'm always happy to see one of my students again," she told him. "Come on in. Would you like some tea and cookies?"

"Sure, that would be delightful," I said. She ran off to the kitchen. We sat down on an old Victorian couch.

Robert said, "She always promised her students a finished painting even if she had to finish it herself. You remember my little painting that I showed you, don't you?"

"Yes, I remember. It was painted quite well."

"I liked coming here to paint and have some time in Nelson. She was a motherly figure for me."

"I can see why you would come here to paint. She's a very loving lady."

They reminisced for a while and then we said our goodbyes. I admired that this eighty-year-old woman was able to earn a living and make so many young people happy. I thought about how that might be a possibility for me in the distant future. Unlike most of my friends, I obsessed a bit about how I would take care of myself when I get older.

The next morning, we took a ferry over to Swami Radha's Ashram. It was nestled in trees at the lake's edge. Once we checked in, a disciple showed me to a room that looked comfortable, clean and well organized. Robert had gone off to his room, but soon found me, and suggested that we take a nap after traveling all morning. A while later, we took a stroll around the quiet and serene ashram's grounds.

That evening, Swami Radha called everyone together for satsang. We sang uplifting songs, she gave an inspirational lecture, and we all ate dinner together. I imagined how it would be beneficial for my soul to spend a longer period of time here. Swami Radha had invited me to take her three-month Yoga Development Course, but my business partner Ron had already told me that there was no way I could leave work for more than two weeks. It was too much work for one of us to sustain the business. So, I could only dream of it.

The next morning during our relationship workshop, we were each given a series of questions. For example, we were asked what we expected of each other, and what our individual needs were. Robert and I seemed to be in sync. Then he went off to talk with Terrance, one of Swami's disciples at the ashram and I went off with Swami Tara.

Then Swami Tara asked, "Irene, are there any lingering issues you want resolved?"

"Well," I said, "Robert didn't like me marking maps when we travel, but I have a simple solution. I feel stupid for not having thought of it before. Emotions sure get in the way of thinking clearly."

"Oh, here are Robert and Terrance, now. Why don't you tell him about it."

Excitedly, I said, "Robert I resolved our map problem. I'll buy two maps and I'll mark mine in yellow and keep yours pristine."

He stared at me and said angrily, "That doesn't resolve anything."

Terrance, Swami Tara, and I all looked perplexed. Feeling shocked, I thought, *I'm in trouble*. Then I thought, *maybe give him a break, maybe being at the ashram has brought up some old resentment that he had buried*.

Terrance asked, "Robert, do you want to discuss this?"

Robert said, "No, I'm through for the day. I want to show Irene around the ashram and go for a hike before dinner."

He grabbed my hand and proceeded to show me some of the buildings he'd helped build in earlier years. He was proud of the work he'd done there, though he revealed that he thought he should've been compensated when he'd last left the ashram. His face was red, tightening his grip on my hand. Gently, I pulled my hand away from his.

I said, "It says in her brochure that you are welcome to volunteer services while you live at the ashram. You were fed, had a place to stay, and took classes, right?"

"Yes, but I still think I deserved to earn money."

As we walked along, he pointed to an area, saying, "This is where I would organize and direct the visitor's children to put on impromptu plays, entertaining the adults." Glowing, he added, "That was my favorite job."

It surprised me because he'd so readily got a vasectomy when I told him I didn't want to have children. Feeling stunned, I stopped in my tracks. Reflecting a moment, he said, "Oh, I don't need to have children of my own, I just liked helping them to learn and have fun." I let out a sigh of relief.

I didn't mention the maps again, but I bought two maps anytime we were going to travel somewhere. He accepted our new way of navigating.

CHAPTER EIGHT

Seeking Essences of Spirit

*T*HROUGH ROBERT AND OTHER friends, we continued creating a spiritual community. During the previous ten years that Robert had lived in Swami Radha's spiritual ashram, he'd met quite a few swamis who'd traveled there to give spiritual lectures. One of these teachers that Robert introduced me to was Swami Sahajananda, who lived in Toronto, Canada. He came and stayed with us for two weeks or more each year. Swami loved to tell jokes until we couldn't stop laughing. Slowly, he'd start to interject beautiful spiritual stories. Robert and I invited friends and acquaintances to come to the house to listen to Swami's spiritual lectures. Beforehand, Swami and I prayed and chanted while making a large pot of vegetable curry stew. He told me that the chanting helped us to maintain a vibration of love while cooking, so that such love became part of the food's life force. Then we would serve the love-imbued vegetable stew to our guests after his lecture.

Swami and I sang Swami Yogananda's songs together. He taught me different meditation practices. He had a brilliant mind, reciting different ancient Hindu stories, stating their deeper meanings. Often, all this while we drank coffee in a café.

Fig. 16 Irene and Swami Sahajananda in Laguna Beach, CA

Fig. 17 Irene and Swami Sahajananda are at the Self-Realization Fellowship Lake Shrine Temple

After work, I started taking esoteric classes at The Helix Center, which was located halfway between the jewelry store and home. Robert didn't usually get home from school until late, so I signed up for various classes that would help me to better connect with Spirit.

I took my first hatha yoga class with a wonderful lady named EJ, who taught with a vibrant enthusiasm. During that very first class, while doing a yoga asana, my heart burst open with love. I was hooked on yoga. As I continued with the yoga classes, aches and pains left my physical body. I felt a new deep inner peace.

One night at yoga class, EJ introduced the class to Swami Shantanand. He gave us a demonstration of advanced yoga asanas (postures) and then told us about the Jana Yoga lectures (yoga of the intellect) he gave weekly. A widening spiritual family grew from going to his lectures.

Around the same time, during tai chi classes, heightened sensations of energy flowed through my body, creating a new experience for me. I noticed more synchronicities happening. When I would wish to gain some kind of information, a person would appear with it. I surmised that the new vibration I felt from yoga, and the flowing energy I felt from tai chi, had created an energy field with which I could more easily attract my heart's desires, especially when they were directed to the growth of my spirit and for the highest good of everyone.

An enthusiastic, petite woman, Susan Christopher Ph.D. offered a class in shamanic journeying. I delved into the process. A shamanic journey is when the spirit leaves the shaman's body with the intention of healing another spirit. He/she becomes an intermediary between the physical and spiritual worlds, mostly to heal illness and resolve spiritual or energetic problems. It can also be done for personal healing, spiritual growth, and to connect with nature.

Indigenous shamans used different methods to induce trance states that freed their spirits, such as, special drum beating, ingesting entheogenic (psychoactive) plant helpers or fungi, or by using special breathing and meditation techniques.

Often a shaman's spirit travels down a metaphysical hole in the earth, sometimes arriving at a magical place where they can find power objects, power animals, healing herbs, and healing knowledge. Other times, a shaman journeys down into his body, or even into the body of his client, finding what needs to be healed and how to heal it. An entranced shaman can shape-shift into a Jaguar or a power animal in order to find healing herbs and gain knowledge of the jungle or his terrain. Animal helpers can help find information and healing herbs in realms that aren't normally accessible.

During one of our group journeys, the rhythmic drumming along with a guided meditation took me into an underworld, or actually, what seemed like a voyage into my body. I traveled down long tunnels, feeling as if I were inside my arteries. At the end of the tunnel appeared a colorful magical garden. A beautiful sleek black Jaguar brushed by me. I shivered. He bowed his head, offering me a ride. I mounted him as one would mount a horse. Feeling the Jaguar's muscles against my legs, somehow made me feel powerful with this new alliance. A knowingness of instinctive and primal power was becoming a part of me. He carried me around the garden and into a cave. I saw a sparkling green emerald sitting atop a small mound of gemstones. I slid off the Jaguar's back, bent down, and picked up the stone, holding it close to my heart. I envisioned its energetic essence imprinting my heart. This green stone symbolized *universal truth*, which to me, simultaneously meant *cosmic love*.

A fast-paced drumbeat guided our spirits back up into our bodies. After that, we danced with our power animals, imagining their finer attributes, empowering our psyches. Later on, whenever life became scary or challenging, I summoned up the finer attributes of my power animal for support.

After a few months of teaching us the shamanic journeying classes, Susan Christopher, being a multi-talented teacher, switched gears and offered a sixteen-week class titled "Living Through Possibility Thinking." She was a perfect mentor since I wanted every aspect of my life and art to focus on possibility and solution. She taught us ways to analyze our individual self and abilities to set realistic goals. She also taught us communication skills, relationship skills and speaking skills.

Susan was outrageously humorous. One night when we checked in to tell how our week went, Susan said, "So I had an interesting day today. I went for a job interview for a special project. I arrived a few minutes late because I had had an emergency with my son, whose land was being taken away from him at gunpoint by the locals in Costa Rica."

Susan could hardly contain her laughter, but she continued, "I could see that the interviewer was looking grumpy, so I asked if he could just give me a few minutes and he would see how well suited I was for the position. He agreed to give me a half hour. I thought the interview went well. At the end, he said he had an important meeting to go to and we shook hands. I noticed this long thread hanging from his shirt near his shoulder. So, I stopped him and said, 'You don't want to go into the meeting like this.' I pulled the thread to break it off, but the thread kept coming and his sleeve fell down his arm. Oh my God, the look on the man's face, I was in shock along with him, but I couldn't stop laughing. He ran out of the room. So, I don't think I got the job." Our group laughed for fifteen minutes at her story.

That night Susan taught us about crisis and change.

Susan asked, "How much physical pain or mental pain does it take for you to make a change in your life? How deeply will you allow yourself to sink into a depression? How sick do you have to get before you take care of yourself?"

After sharing we realized that we all had different thresholds, especially before we considered something a crisis.

Susan asked, "How would your life be different if you could feel your discomfort or your pain sooner?"

I said, "Well, we could prevent ourselves from being sick or at least shorten the length of the time we are sick. We could be more efficient in our lives and come to solutions sooner. If we noticed we were depressed or sad, we would do what it took to pull ourselves out of it."

Susan said, "Yes, instead of wallowing in the problems, we would be looking for solutions. We also wouldn't get stuck telling people the same old story about ourselves."

Our assignment was to watch our thoughts and our degrees of emotion, especially the ones that brought sadness or might limit us and see how aware we could be to change our thoughts.

Partly because of Susan's teachings, I showed up at my jewelry store much happier than in the past. My business partner Ron wanted to know what I was doing. I told him about Susan and he signed up for her next set of classes.

Ron became so inspired, he began holding a weekly healing group at his house. He was on his path of greater self-awareness. When we were married, it was pretty much just he and I, barely a social life.

All these esoteric experiences gave me a deeper understanding of my mind-body-self. They connected me with the essence of ancient cultures. And by creating a harmony or attunement in my life they were contributing to the growth of our business.

I had asked the universe for images and visions of love that I could paint. The universe sent me many loving people to show me aspects of love. And so it was.

CHAPTER NINE

Delving into Dreams

DREAMS CAN MAKE FRIGHTENING, threatening images. One night, after roiling in chaotic terrifying images conjured up from the depths of my psyche, I awoke in my bed. Deep indigo shadows swallowed the room. Sweat glued the bed sheet to my body. Chills ran down my spine. Bits of the dream images came to me of a dog pulling and biting at my fingers. I wondered if I would ever be able to sleep again? This was not the only dream that tortured my childhood. I'd also had a reoccurring dream of rats biting me while I was sleeping within the dream.

These nightmares can be traced back to two events. One of these dreams came after a dog bit me on my head when I was three years old. I remember it so clearly: One extremely hot and humid morning, Mom, my sister Ruth and I were walking to grandma's house. As I spied a German Shepherd sitting on the sidewalk outside a local bar, I shook my hand free from my sister's sweaty hand. She was only too happy to let go. As mom and Ruth trudged ahead of me, I opened my arms to give the dog a hug. As we were eye to eye, he bared his teeth, snarling with a low growl. I stopped in my tracks, thinking he just needs a hug. As I quickly hugged him, he bit me on my head. Feeling pain and screaming, while warm blood dripped down my face, I ran to catch up with my mom and sister.

"Oh, my God," Mom exclaimed, as she looked back and saw the dog barking at us. Ruth, you were supposed to be holding your sister's hand! What are we going to do? Her head is bleeding."

We were about to cross the street when a policeman stopped his car because he heard me crying. His face looked startled. From his car seat, he peered at us. "What happened?"

Mom pointed her finger. "That dog bit her. What should we do?"

Jumping out of his car, he said, "Those bar dogs are trained to attack and stop fights."

As he inspected my head, he continued, "She needs stitches to stop the bleeding. Get in my car and I'll take you and your children to the hospital."

Off we went to the hospital. I recovered quickly. After that, however, when a dog snarled at me, I took it seriously. Those bad dog dreams haunted me into my twenties.

The other recurring nightmare came after what started out as a seemingly innocent event. The family piled excitedly into Uncle Al's prized Cadillac. We arrived at the fairgrounds with a cacophony of sounds drowning out our conversations. A man called us to thrills and excitement. For a nickel, we were enticed into a tent where we could see an exhibit of unprecedented historical tortures that people had inflicted on one another. We hesitated, but curiosity got the better of us. My sisters, Ruth and Jayne, my brother Ed, and I handed the man our nickels.

The lighting was eerie inside the tent with only the exhibits illuminated. There was a large painting of a man screaming as he was torn apart by horses. Wooden constructions were designed to hold men while townspeople tortured them. Stunned, I stopped in my tracks at an exhibit that showed a man held down by a wooden contraption in a small room while being eaten alive by rats. I had seen violence in my short little life of seven years, but nothing seemed this cruel.

Shivering and scared out of my mind I ran over to Ruth and asked, "Is this true, can people be this cruel?"

Ruth said, "I hope this isn't true."

On the verge of tears, I said, "Ruth, I don't want to see any more, can we get out of here?"

Ruth called, "Hey you guys, Irene and I are going to head over to the roller coaster. Do you want to come?

Ed and Jayne said, "Yea, let's get out of here."

Because of these bad dreams when some of my college peers told me how they had recurring bad dream hallucinations from LSD and other drugs, I decided that my bad dreams were good enough reason for me not to partake. I thought life was tough enough, so why add to the drudgery. And since I had my near-death experience at age nine, I valued my mind and I didn't want to risk damaging it. Also, I knew that my imagination was already too powerful.

I chose not to take LSD mainly because I didn't feel the need, but I'm open to all experiences that lead to greater soul development. A lot of my friends had beautiful visions and life enhancing experiences from entheogenic plant substances and fungi. Some of their art is very beautiful and soulful. I believe when these entheogenic concoctions are taken with sacred intent, one's chance for an enhanced experience is heightened. I also honor the spiritual traditions of indigenous people to use their plant helpers.

I was tempted, but my bad dreams were a deterrent, and so I prayed to God/the Goddess to please give me powerful visions naturally. I remained open to taking these substances should the right moment have presented itself. I'd also like to point out that some extremely soulful and beautiful art has been made by artists who tap into the universe through meditation, breathing techniques, contemplation, sound, and their deep heartfelt connection to nature, humanity and the universe.

I could understand why many people choose not to remember their dreams. But nightmares made me want to explore dreams; I needed a healing and sensed there was more to these nighttime dramas. The bible and other historical stories told of people having dreams of foretelling the future. And I occasionally had had dreams of designing clothing and waking up happy.

During my first year in college in Psychology class, the teacher mentioned how Freud had written about dreams, sparking my interest. So, Freud's *Interpretation of Dreams* was the subject of my first term paper. He wrote about how the day's events recreated themselves, sometimes seemingly nonsensical. He wrote that even when a person is in a dream state, outside stimulus, such as wind blowing on a person or the sound of bells ringing influenced the said person's dream. Freud was interesting to me, but I wanted to know more about the magical side of dreaming. Thus, over the years, I kept daily diaries that included significant dreams as well as read books about dream interpretation.

Now it was time to explore dream symbolism even more deeply. In 1984, Robert and I joined the C. G. Jung Club in Orange County and went to their lectures. It was there that I met Pan Koukoklas Ph.D. who was fully versed in Greek myths and other myths from around the world. Robert and I attended his Jungian Dream Analysis group that met once a week for a year and then met every other week for another year. I began writing my dreams almost every day. Similarly, as with my artwork, I would look in my Jungian symbol books for the meanings of the symbols that appeared in my dreams and interpret what they may have been communicating.

As others related their dreams, I soon realized how much spirit (our higher self) really wanted to speak to us and give us guidance. When we are in that quiet state of sleep, it seems, our psyche is more available to listen. I listened week after week to one woman's dreams. She was a self-proclaimed atheist and ran away from the possibility that she had a spirit or that God existed. In her recurring nightmares, a monster was always chasing her. Finally, in a dream, she couldn't take the drama of this monster chasing her and she turned around to face it. She realized it was herself – her spirit. She hugged herself.

As she told us the dream, crying with joy, she said, "I now realize that I have a spirit, that I am spirit, and there is a 'God'."

Her experience made me even more determined to listen to my dreams. And as I paid attention to them, they made waking life more fascinating. Dreams led me on journeys. Some dreams were archetypal, their images and symbols having similar meanings through past eons of time. These archetypal symbols connected me to my psyche, helping to raise my consciousness and in seeing the oneness of humanity.

Reading a book often inspired my dreams, which in turn inspired my life. After going to a lecture on a book titled, *The Book of Knowledge: The Keys of Enoch*, by J. J. Hurtak, I purchased the book, a highly esoteric channeled text explaining the 'Energetic Light' and evolutionary process of the universal soul through eons. It explained how the earth has energetic grids holding sacred knowledge for our collective spiritual evolution. Many of these energy centers are at pyramids around the world. The book listed a group of Mayan ruins that were important centers for maintaining the sacred grid.

While the book seemed far beyond my comprehension, most of its words rang true to my heart. I questioned the story explaining the process of spiritual evolution as a hierarchy and that a patriarchal formula was a universal truth. My heart felt there was more to the story than he or I was able to comprehend.

However, shortly after reading part of the book, I dreamt I was in a Mayan pyramid temple located on a hill. I could see a city-complex of pyramids around me surrounded by a vast jungle. I felt peaceful. I felt at home. In the dream, as I stood up from meditating, I stared at carved stone images on the wall before me.

A voice said, "Irene, slowly move your hands over the images and you will know our language, you will intuit our knowledge."

AWAKENING LOVE'S VIBRATIONS

The next morning, I pondered the dream. While talking with Robert at breakfast, I told him that I needed to travel to the Mayan ruins, especially Palenque, Mexico. So, we planned our first of many trips to the Mayan ruins.

Fig. 18 Irene is in a purple skirt, standing atop Temple of the Warriors, near Chac Mool with serpent heads behind her. Chichen Itza, Mexico

Fig. 19 Robert is standing atop the Jaguar and Eagle Temple with the Temple of Kukulkan in the distance. Chichen Itza pyramids, Yucatan, Mexico in 1987.

CHAPTER TEN

The Mayan Ruins

THE DAY OF OUR TRIP ARRIVED. After the stopover in Mexico City, we traveled first to Merida, a city located near the ruins of Mayapan. Then we traveled to Uxmal, Kabah, Chichen Itza, and Palenque. At each of these ancient sites, I took time to be quiet, feel the energies, and say prayers.

Each pyramid complex had its own artistic motif, its own energetic feeling, and its own mysteries. In Chichen Itza, I was fascinated by a stone carving of a giant serpent head at the base of the north face of Castle pyramid (also known as Temple of Kukulkan). On March 21st of each year, the spring equinox, the sun sets, and forms an undulating shadow on the pyramid's stairs, connecting to the serpent's head. This gives the appearance that the snake is moving down the stairs. From the snake's apparent movement, winter transforms into spring. This was when the Maya planted their crops and performed their spring ceremonies. Now, people come from all over the world to watch this magic on this particular day of the year and to experience the sacred energy of this ceremonial complex.

Fig. 20 Chac Mool in Chichen Itza, Mexico

Fig. 21 Left - Irene is standing at La Iglesia Temple decorated with elaborated masks of Chaac, the Rain God.
Fig. 22 Right – One of the serpent heads at the base of the pyramid stairs at Chichen-Itza, Mexico.

So many questions arose in me. I was just beginning to understand these different energies now moving through my body. They vibrated within my physical form, harmonizing it with a higher source. This sacred site acted like a tuning fork. I wondered, *Did all the sacred ceremonies from the past leave their vibration blueprint in the air? I knew from visiting some ancient churches in Europe that there was an incredible feeling of peace inside them, perhaps residual from all the sincere prayers and ceremonies of past peoples. Or was it that sensitive souls found natural high-vibration sites at which to build these pyramids, churches and temples? Is it a vibration attunement that connects us to our divine source? Where did all these people go?*

I had learned in Europe, as well as other places in the world, that many churches were built over earlier temples and pagan sites of worship. Even the ninety-foot tall pyramid, the Temple of Kukulkan, the Feathered Serpent God built during the eleventh to thirteen centuries was built over the foundations of previous temples.

Mayan temples were also used for observing the stars and the passages of time. The Temple of Kukulkan was connected to our yearly calendar. Each side of the pyramid has ninety-one steps. With the platform (4 sides x 91 steps + platform = 365 days) it equals the number of days in a year. The pyramid is directionally oriented to mark equinoxes and solstices. And inside of the El Caracol observatory in Chichen Itza, the doors and windows along the spiraling staircase ascend and are aligned with astrological movements, primarily the path of Venus.

At Palenque, I was like a child who had just arrived home. It was a huge ceremonial complex surrounded by rainforest. It was a hot humid day with mosquitoes searching everywhere for human blood. That wasn't going to slow me down. I was determined to climb to the top of every pyramid. I ran from temple to temple climbing sideways up the steep narrow steps, viewing the rest of the complex, meditating, and sitting quietly for a few minutes atop of each pyramid. Most tourists came by in groups and only climbed a few of the pyramids, so I often got to sit alone on top of the pyramids while enjoying the scenery below.

Finally, I saw the temple that had appeared in my dream. It was unusual looking and had a triangular opening above the open rectangular doorway. The roof had open triangular shapes with an open circle above them. This building stood at the edge of the complex, near the jungle. Making my way up the steep stairs, I was amazed to see the original stele (carvings) on the walls. When no one was around, I gently ran my hands over the carved images to receive the information they had hidden inside of them. I barely touched them because I didn't want to damage this beautiful imagery, believing that just being near it was enough to receive its vibrations. I sat there quietly, emptying my mind of thought. This temple felt as though it had been a home for me in the distant past.

Suddenly, loud roaring sounds, like those of a ferocious jaguar, rang out of the encroaching jungle. Shivers of fear shot through my body. A passing tourist laughed when he saw the expression on my face.

He said, "Those are Howler monkeys."

"Are you sure those are monkey sounds?"

"Yes, our tour guide told us about them."

"Well, that just makes me more scared, because now how will I know if a real Jaguar is approaching or not?"

"Jaguars don't usually come around the ruins until dusk. Besides, a Jaguar would… most likely … silently sneak up on you and have your throat in his jaws before you know what has happened."

Laughing with a bit of trepidation, I said, "Thanks a lot."

"No problem," he said, flashing a big smile.

He made his way slowly down the tall narrow steps of the pyramid. I stood up and scanned the vast complex of pyramids, searching the encroaching jungle for signs of animal life. I calmed myself down and meditated some more and then continued exploring the complex.

As dusk fell, I found Robert about to ascend another pyramid.

I yelled, "Hey Robert, let's go. It's closing time."

"Let's not leave until they make us," he yelled back.

Not wanting him to know that I was scared of a Jaguar showing up, I said, "The mosquitoes are going to come in droves soon."

"Okay, we'll come back first thing in the morning," he said.

The next morning, Robert and I climbed the Temple of Inscriptions. It's supposed to be the only Mayan pyramid with a tomb inside. Once on top, we descended the narrow stairway inside the temple to glimpse Pacal Votan's tomb and the famous lid for his sarcophagus. In *Chariots of the Gods*, the author, Erick von Daniken said that it looks as though Pacal Votan were in a space suit implying he may have come to Earth from another planet. I surmised that anything is possible, and decided to later seek other people's thoughts on that subject. This was one of the few pyramids in America known to have a king buried in it. The imagery did look like Pacal Votan had worn a space suit. *Or was it a symbolic breathing suit for his spirit?* I had so many questions.

Fig. 23 Palenque Ruins - Temple of the Foliated Cross is the small one in the middle, with triangular openings above the doorway and windows above the first level, which is the temple that appeared in my dream.

As we climbed back up the inside the temple stairs, I said, "Robert, I have to go visit my dream temple once more before we leave."

"Okay, I'll meet up with you later."

Once again, I climbed the narrow steps to the summit of my favorite temple, Temple of the Foliated Cross. I sat and meditated for a while. It felt so good to be sitting there basking in the sunshine. I was in a sweet reverie when I noticed the sun setting behind the luscious green jungle. Hurriedly, I jumped up and ran to find Robert so we could leave.

That evening, a group of gentle, white-robed people, appearing to be from an ancient time had gathered near the exit gate. They were selling art of Mayan images burnt into pieces of leather.

Browsing the images, I asked the artist, "Are you from a local tribe?"

Gently he replied, "Yes, we are the direct descendants of the Mayans, the Lacandoni. We live in a village in the surrounding rainforest."

I purchased three pieces of the leather art, then tentatively, I asked, "Have you been able to keep alive your people's ancient knowledge?"

He studied my face, and said, "Yes, there are keepers of our ancient knowledge."

Feeling a harmonious connection, I said, "Thanks so much for the beautiful artwork. Blessings to you."

"Blessings to you, young lady. Have a safe journey."

Fig. 24 Another view of temples at Palenque.

On our way back to the states, Robert and I spent three days in Mexico City. Our first stop was at the National Museum of Anthropology. After traveling to all those pyramid sites, it was wonderful to view the museum's featured time-line of the various indigenous cultures and their images, all showing the rich historic magnificence of Mexico. After spending a day and a half there, we moved on and visited Siqueiros's murals and the Tamayo Museum. I embraced the Mexican artists for their extremely passionate expression of politics, psychology, and life.

While sitting in a café drinking coffee, I said, "Robert, this has been one of our most adventurous trips. For our next trip, I would love to see the pyramids in Tikal, Guatemala."

He smiled and nodded his head, "That would be exciting."

AWAKENING LOVE'S VIBRATIONS

Fig. 25 Irene is standing in front of Siqueiros's mural.

CHAPTER ELEVEN

Dreaming and The Dalai Lama Initiation

UPON ARRIVING HOME from the Mayan trip, I continued taking esoteric classes after work and on Saturdays. My knowledge of symbols, myths, and dreams deepened. Some dreams were a confused mixture of experiences from an exhausting day of work. Others were more significant. Sometimes my dreams were very clear, even saying, "Irene if you just do such and such, you'll have a fine day." Dreams were becoming a great part of my life. I thought of my paintings as 'crystallized dreams', the images channeled onto the canvas through my hands and brushes.

One evening I had a lucid archetypal dream. The dream had a *substance* and felt very real. I dreamt I was walking through a garden filled with large art sculptures. *Oh, these could be my sculptures,* I thought. As I walked through the garden, a force exploded up through the earth and blew me into the sky. My clothes were blown off my body! A huge eagle flew by and caught me, taking me to its nest. I was the same size as its babies. The baby eagles were crying for sustenance. The mother eagle brought back food, but there was nothing edible for me, so I crawled out of the nest and down the mountainside. As I was retracing my steps back through the sculpture garden, a sudden wind swirled and blew me into a long shallow cave. Inside the cave stood a rectangular wooden table with benches carved from a tree's sides. At the far end of the table stood two Tibetan monks wearing orange robes and pointed hats.

One of the monks held his arm straight out, pointed to me and, in an authoritative voice, said, "I'm to be your teacher."

"Okay," I said.

The next morning, when I awoke, I asked Robert, "Have you ever seen any Tibetan men wearing pointed hats? There were two such men in my dream."

He said, "I have a book that shows the Dalai Lama in a pointed ceremonial hat."

As Robert searched for the book, I said, "Yesterday, after work, I was listening to a Tibetan Chant record album, feeling an affinity to the Tibetan monks. On the cover, they showed a picture of a temple and I was imagining what it might be like to be a monk. That might have caused me to have the dream."

Robert found the book and showed me a picture of the Dalai Lama in a pointed hat.

"Wow, Robert, that's the person in my dream. He said that he's to be my teacher. I wonder what that means?"

Robert replied, "Maybe you'll meet him someday. You might want to read this book."

"I'm running late, I have to rush to get to our special breakfast meeting at the Ritz-Carlton hotel. See you later."

I arrived just in the nick of time. Ron didn't like me being late. He would often remind me that there was no such thing as being *on time*; you were either early or late. Be here early, his words rang in my mind. When we made our monthly store sale's goal, we would have our breakfast meeting at the Ritz-Carlton Hotel, which emanated luxury and money.

I loved eating at the Ritz. It was such a beautiful place, overlooking the Pacific Ocean. It made me appreciate the finer things that money could buy, inspiring me to work hard.

After the breakfast meeting ended, Sheila, our store manager, tapped me on the shoulder. "Irene, I'm not sure why I did this, but I was talking to my friend at the Bodhi Tree bookstore in LA yesterday, and he told me that the Dalai Lama is giving a Three-Day Initiation at the Scottish Rite Masonic Temple in LA this weekend. He told me he had two tickets left. I reserved one for you."

Surprised, I replied, "Thanks. The Dalai Lama is to be my teacher. He came to me in my dream last night, Sheila. I'm pretty sure I'm supposed to be there."

We drove our cars back to Zia Jewelry. We had to get the jewelry out of the safes and displayed in the glass showcases. Once we had the store doors open for business, I followed Ron into the back room.

"Ron," I said. "I know this is kind of short notice, but I need Sunday off from work. I want to go to LA for a Three-Day Initiation. It's really important to me. I'll do a make-up day for you, when you need one."

Ron, with his mind focused on finding something in the large jewelry safe, replied, "I don't have anything special planned this Sunday, so you're in luck."

I looked forward to this mysterious initiation of three days. It finally arrived.

During the conference, the Dalai Lama told us about divine virtues, clarity and kindness. He talked about different types of dreaming. He told us how a spiritual teacher could astral-project himself into the dream or the waking life of his disciple in order to teach, help, heal, or encourage the disciple. I was amazed by the Dalai Lama's stories.

We were told to give something up as a sacrifice before the initiation, even if it was easy for us to do so. I gave up drinking alcohol. I only drank a few times a year in celebration, anyway, and I was already questioning that behavior. After just one drink my mind would feel foggy for a few days. I'd feel *Blah*. Drinking alcohol usually gave me an immediate headache, so I took a vow to give it up.

Then the Dalai Lama lectured that we were not to break our vows, even in our dreams. That night, I dreamt I was drinking wine. I woke up the next morning upset. *How'll I take my initiation*?

That morning, the Dalai Lama said, "I want you to know that your mind is tricky. Some of you broke your vows in your dreams last night."

People in the audience laughed. *Thank God, I wasn't the only one.*

He said, "Now everyone who wants to be initiated will retake his or her vow."

It was a momentous day for me. I learned a lot more about dreams and about the symbolic nature of Buddhism. We wore blindfolds and took a guided journey into a Sacred Mandala. A Mandala is a circular form, symbolizing the way to our center, to our spirit. It can use symbolic imagery such as deities, Buddha, and dragon guards. It is often combined with the Yantra, a sacred geometric diagram, whose imagery is also used for contemplation, inducing mental states and guiding our spirit to move forward on its evolutionary journey.

During a break, I met Ed, who revealed to me that he had traveled to the sacred Mayan ruins, planting crystals at the sacred sites to reinforce the energetic grid of Mother Earth. He told me the esoteric "Arc-Angel Brotherhood" was directing him. I told him that a dream had put me on a similar path.

Ed had also traveled to sacred sites around the world following astrological eclipse lines and burying crystals along those lines. After the conference, we met for lunch. He told me stories of the sacred history of places he had traveled. I sat there mesmerized. I thought, *It's interesting that when Ed travels he focuses and discovers the "sacred history" of towns in those countries. If only the history books in our schools considered other powerful aspects of life rather than just wars and the materialistic aspects of our society.*

"One of the Easiest Ways for Your Divine-Self to Speak with You is Through Your Dreams."

Irene Vincent

CHAPTER TWELVE

Trip to Esalen for Psychosynthesis

I NEVER KNEW WHERE the next divine lesson might come from. For a few months, I had been contemplating the words *judgment* and *discrimination*. I didn't feel as if I were coming to any understanding of those words. Then, while I was visiting my friends Don and Donna, they told me that they were to driving to Esalen, CA. to take a psychosynthesis workshop taught by a psychologist named Harry Sloan. The class was about union of the mind, body, and soul. It was mainly designed for therapists and psychologists. I asked if I could go with them. They were delighted.

That following week, we drove on a narrow coastal road along windy cliffs that hung high above the Pacific Ocean. Life's paradox pervaded. My mouth hung agape, while my heart expanded with a joyousness at seeing the great expansive ocean sparkling trillions of lights as if carrying in continuance the night sky into day. The water's changing hues of turquoises and lapis blues flickered by. Monolithic rocks jutted up out of the ocean conjuring images of ancient times. And at the same time, my stomach muscles contracted as I clutched the front seat bracing myself, for one wrong turn and the car could plummet hundreds of feet.

As we got closer to Esalen Institute the forest trees grew right up to the edges of the road, giving me a protected feeling. Soon, we arrived. Don and Donna shared a private room, and I shared an upstairs room in the same house with two other women. The class was being held downstairs in a large room in the same house.

During Sloan's class, we went through a lot of different practices and exercises. For one of the exercises, the dance therapy instructor arrived late. She explained that she was a bit late and tired because, at fifty years old, she had just been blessed with the birth of twins. She had never used birth control and had never conceived before.

As she demonstrated a freeform dance, she transformed before our eyes. All the energy came back into her body and she looked beautiful. I had already started freeform dancing in the morning as I got myself ready for work. I turned on the music that I had waiting in the tape player. I called it a trigger. The moment I heard the music, I automatically started dancing. I incorporated some of the Tai Chi and Yoga stretches, relieving myself of pain. I thought of it as dancing through the pain, creating beauty. She reminded me how simple and fun it was to replenish my energy: Just *start dancing*.

I also did this *music trigger* when a painting took several sessions. I played one main piece of music and when I stood before my painting in progress, I remembered my thoughts of where I left off.

In another session Harry asked, "How many of you paint?"

Four of us raised our hands? He pointed to Sally and asked, "Can you share your process?"

Sally said, "I like to copy things and make them look pretty. And sometimes I just play abstractly with the colors."

"How do you feel during and after the painting process?"

"I feel happy," she said.

Another woman chirped in, "Painting makes me happy, too."

I could see Harry astutely observing my facial expressions going from questioning to pain. "What is the process like for you, Irene?"

"I go through a whole gamut of emotions. I don't always know what image I'm making. I often discover different aspects of myself through the process and then express my feelings in a deep way. I struggle with taking the painting to another technical level, whether through the way I apply the paint, the composition, etc. I wonder if I might express the image in a new way. When I finish a piece of art, sometimes I'm relieved and happy, other times I'm sad that the struggle is over and there are things I need to change in my life."

Harry said, "An artist wants to go beyond what has been expressed before him by other artists, he wants to express something from within and this can feel like a struggle. A great composer and musician wants to create a new sound, a sound he hears in his heart and soul. A great physicist searches to discover something new about the workings of the universe. So as in the art of living, life is not always as happy as we'd like it to be. However, as our mind, body, and soul come into a harmony, we do feel a deep inner peace and joy that is not easily ruffled by life's challenges."

After that session ended, a couple stopped me on our way out the door, and Bob asked, "Irene, did you bring any pictures of your art?"

"Oh yes, I brought my portfolio. Would you like to see it?"

"We collect art. That is, if it's in our price range," replied Jan.

"Okay, how about I bring my portfolio over to the dining room tonight?"

We met that evening and I showed them photographs of my drawings and expressionistic paintings. They bought a pastel drawing called, *Four People in Hunger* drawn in 1981 and *Lady with a Cigarette*, a painting on paper.

Another event occurred at Esalen as Don, Donna, and I were walking in the dark to our house. We saw orange light orbs dancing among the branches of the trees. At first, we thought they were lanterns. As we got within three feet of them, we saw that they were some kind of energetic spheres moving around on their own accord. We decided that Esalen was a magical place.

The next day, I went for a massage, a kind of rolling massage. At one point, in my imagination, the doors of my heart exploded open and shut, again and again until they blew off entirely. At first, I was scared. *I don't have any psychological protection*, I thought. Suddenly, a great peace and joy came over me. I realized my heart could always be open to receive love and to give love. My heart didn't need protection.

Towards the last day, Harry gave us a guided meditation and told us to continue meditating for ten minutes. In my meditation, judgmental thoughts that I had about my life appeared in large lit-up neon letters, flashing across a movie arcade. Some of my self-judging life experiences passed before my mind's eye. I was shocked and embarrassed.

Then a voice spoke, "In everything that you ever have done, you were seeking God. You were seeking your source. I do not judge you. Men judge men. I am Love."

My meditation taught me about the word "judgment." And I learned a lot about the essence of love.

Before we came out of the meditation, Harry slipped a picture in our hands.

"Open your eyes," he said lovingly. "This is a picture of my Guru."

As we looked at the picture, we all started laughing. Some of us rolled on the floor. The picture was of a clothed chimpanzee, smiling and sitting in a chair. Harry wanted to remind us not to live our lives too seriously, and of the healing power of laughter.

Harry had led a very special workshop. Everyone in the group had an experience of the divine, even those that previously claimed to be atheists.

AWAKENING LOVE'S VIBRATIONS

Fig. 26 Robert, Irene, Donna, and Don are loving a big tree.

CHAPTER THIRTEEN

Exploring Shamanism in my Art

AT THE LAGUNA BEACH SCHOOL OF ART, under the tutelage of an innovative teacher named Frank Dixon, I explored the world of the Shaman through the medium of monotypes. Frank would play all kinds of avant-garde music and employ strange props alongside the models in order to stimulate our imaginations. While intertwining dancing and painting, every so often, our class would be reprimanded for having too much fun.

Even though our class was officially a painting class, the art school allowed us to use the printing presses, so long as no printing classes were scheduled at that time. Monotypes are a fast, spontaneous way to paint. After oil painting on a metal plate for two to eight hours, I'd lay a slightly dampened sheet of paper over the painted plate. After figuring the right pressure, the painted-plate and paper were squeezed together from passing through the press's rollers. The oil paint had to still be wet enough to transfer into the fiber of the paper. Usually, only one print could be made, but by spraying turpentine on another sheet of slightly dampened paper and running it through the press, a second print, called a ghost print could be made. It sometimes appeared even nicer than the first one.

One of my first prints *Shaman Dream Dance* (see Fig. 27) was inspired by drumming and shamanic journeying workshops. The dreamer is finding her power spirit through the dance of the dark blue shadow figures. The snake slithering through the left side of the image represents kundalini or spiritual energy awakening within myself. As I explored various conscious-raising classes, snakes appeared in my dreams more and more frequently.

Dream interpretation classes taught me a lot about symbols, aiding me in my personal awakening. Having been raised a Catholic, I had long associated snakes with devious sinister behavior. From the feelings during my dreams, I could tell that association was no longer there.

Medical science's symbol, the staff with the two intertwined snakes, had always been perplexing to me. Now I intuited that the two snakes represented male and female energies. I recognized also that the staff and the two snakes resembled a DNA helix.

In Hindu culture, the snake is symbolic of the kundalini energy coiled at the base of the human spine. It represents latent consciousness, which upon awakening would travel up through the chakras, activating a spin and vibration pattern that vibrated out into the physical cells of the body. This awakening created in the recipient a sense of deep peace, bliss and joy.

AWAKENING LOVE'S VIBRATIONS

    From these new revelations, the snake became a positive symbol. The snake spoke of a powerful awakening already occurring within me. In retrospect, I wondered if the Catholic Church's biased interpretation of snakes was to keep us disempowered.

    Through practicing both tai chi and yoga, I was becoming sensitive to different types of energy pulsing through my body, becoming aware of their healing powers, for others and myself. And by exploring "energy" in an image, it made it visible through expressive brushstrokes and modulated colors.

Fig. 27 Irene Vincent, *Shaman Dream Dance*, 1984, monotype: oil on archival black paper, 24"H x 24"W

Irene Vincent

In my next print, *Cosmic Dance* (see Fig 28), a male and female figure danced in the sky, celebrating life. To get images for this, Robert stood high on a ladder, taking photos of me on the floor, posing as if I were flying. Then I took photos of him. The energy of the brushstrokes and paint pushed around by my fingers created a sense of movement in the piece. This piece is a spiritual symbolic dance of my inner male and female energies.

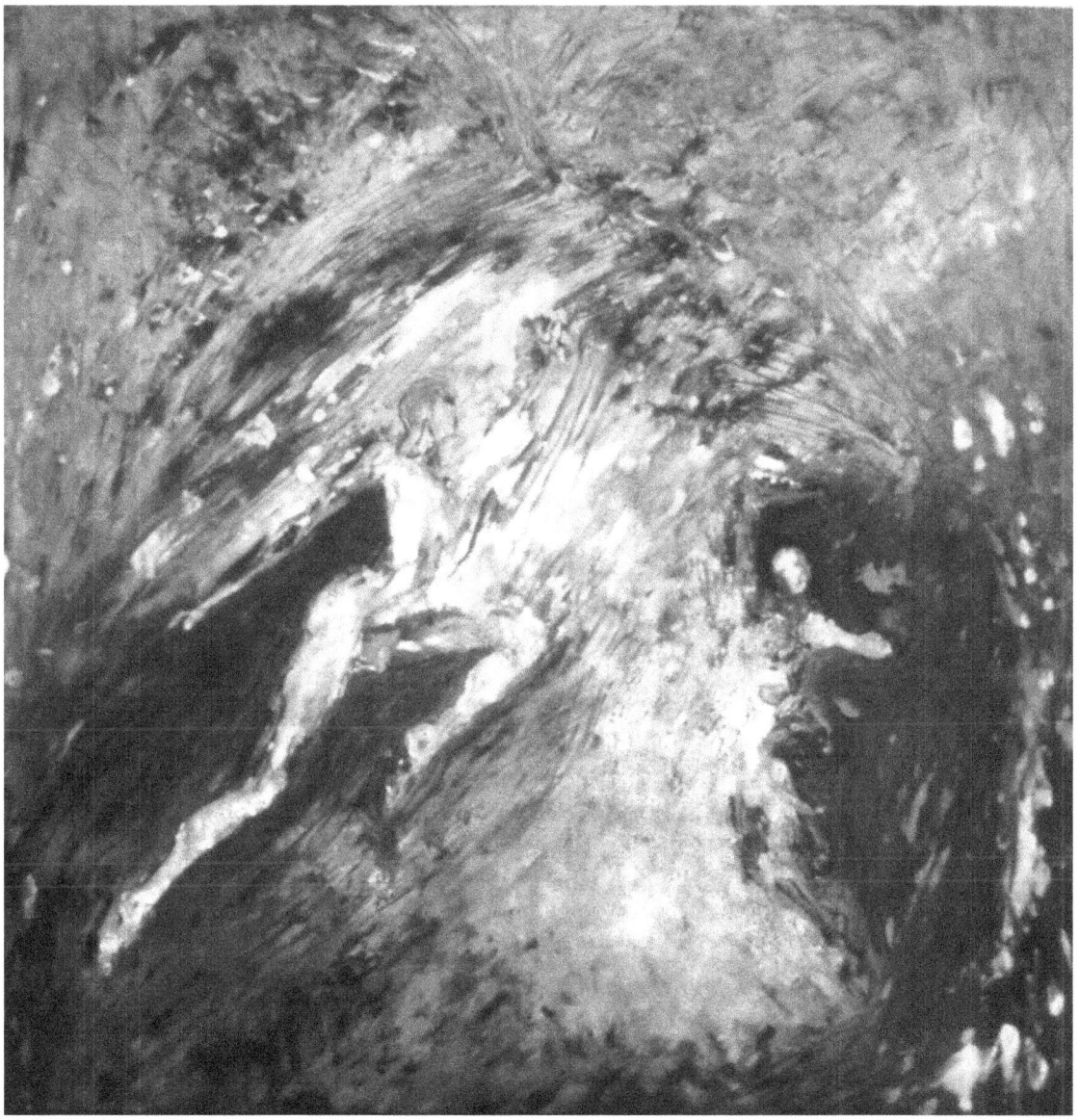

Fig. 28 Irene Vincent, *Cosmic Dance*, 1984, monotype: oil on archival black paper, 30"H x 30"W

AWAKENING LOVE'S VIBRATIONS

In the monotype, *Medicine Woman Speaks* (see Fig.29), the ancient goddess figure is recreated from part of the main image in my painting *Missiles and Coffee Cups* (see Fig. 4). She intrigued me. What was she about? I wanted her to speak. Her upper torso is combined with a spiraling snake bottom, depicting a wise snake goddess with healing powers.

The Goddess's third eye is emphasized with a large diamond shape, symbolizing her connection to the heavens. The diamond shape for her mouth is repeated to emphasize that she speaks from a higher source. Her hands surround her mouth, in order to magnify the volume of her speech, as she floats in space. This brighter print was actually the ghost print or the second print. The more muted, first print was titled *Echoes of Devotion* (see Fig. 30), since I was feeling devoted to the growth of my soul and spirit.

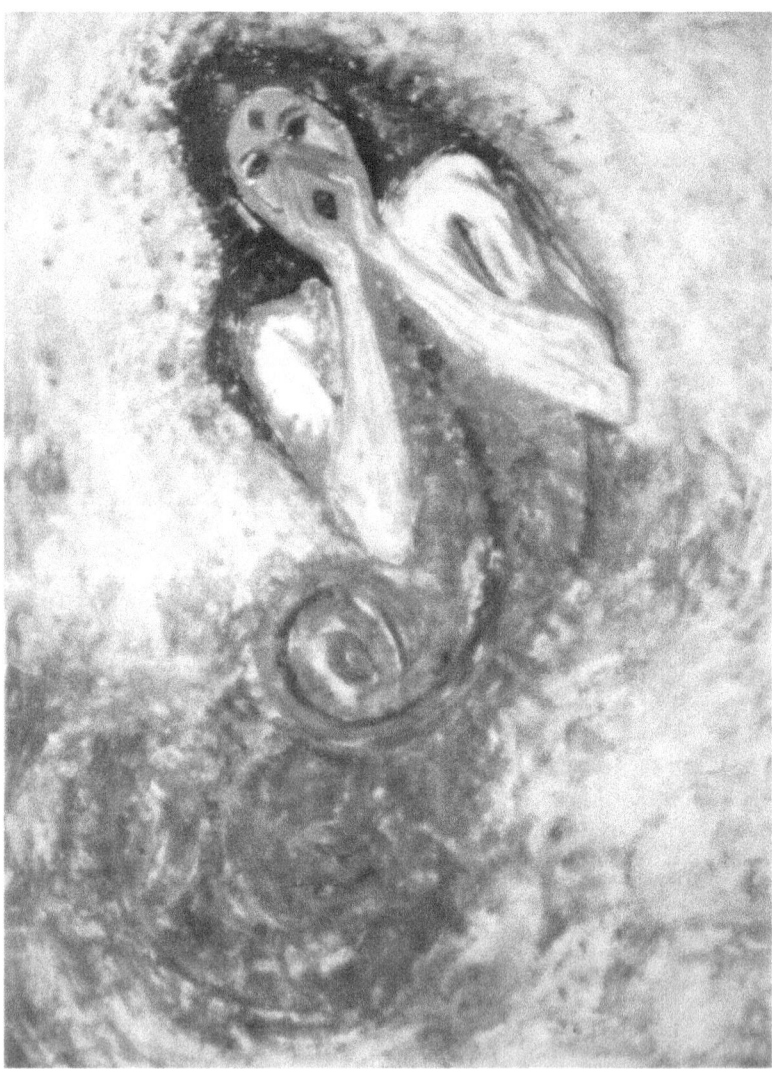

Fig. 29 I. Vincent, *Medicine Woman Speaks*, 1985, monotype: oil on archival paper, 24"H x 18"W

Irene Vincent

Fig. 30 Irene Vincent, *Echoes of Devotion*, 1985, monotype: oil on archival paper, 24"H x 18"W

In the monotype, *Some Enchanted Meeting* (see Fig. 31) the flying plumed serpent is meeting the humming bird. The plumed serpent, Quetzalcoatl, with its feathered head, is symbolic of both, Heaven and Earth. The three coils in the snake's body reveals its spiritual qualities. The humming bird represents the heavens, since it flies in the sky. In Native American tradition, it is a messenger of good news, probably since it drinks the nectar of flowers. Strange, otherworldly red rock formations loom out of the water, which merges with the sky. In this image, my psyche is exploring the marriage of opposites, of the spiritual and the material.

AWAKENING LOVE'S VIBRATIONS

Fig. 31 Irene Vincent, *Some Enchanted Meeting*, 1985, monotype: oil on archival paper, 18"H x 24"W

A year earlier, before I knew there was a butterfly posture in hatha yoga, I had a friend take photographs of me in such a pose, as well as other poses. I wanted my own heartfelt poses from which to do drawings and paintings.

In order to protect my hands, while painting oils on the metal plates, I started wearing rubber gloves and, at times, thin cotton gloves. It just seemed easier to move paint around with my fingers instead of brushes. Like an eraser technique, the cloth gloves gave me more control in wiping paint off the plate. *Butterfly Woman* (see Fig. 32) was painted very spontaneously, while I tried to capture the feeling I had felt in my body during the pose.

The second print felt airy and light, connecting me to my inner being, so I called it *Inner Spaces* (see Fig. 33). Through making these monotype images, it seemed as if my psyche were preparing me for an unusual spiritual future.

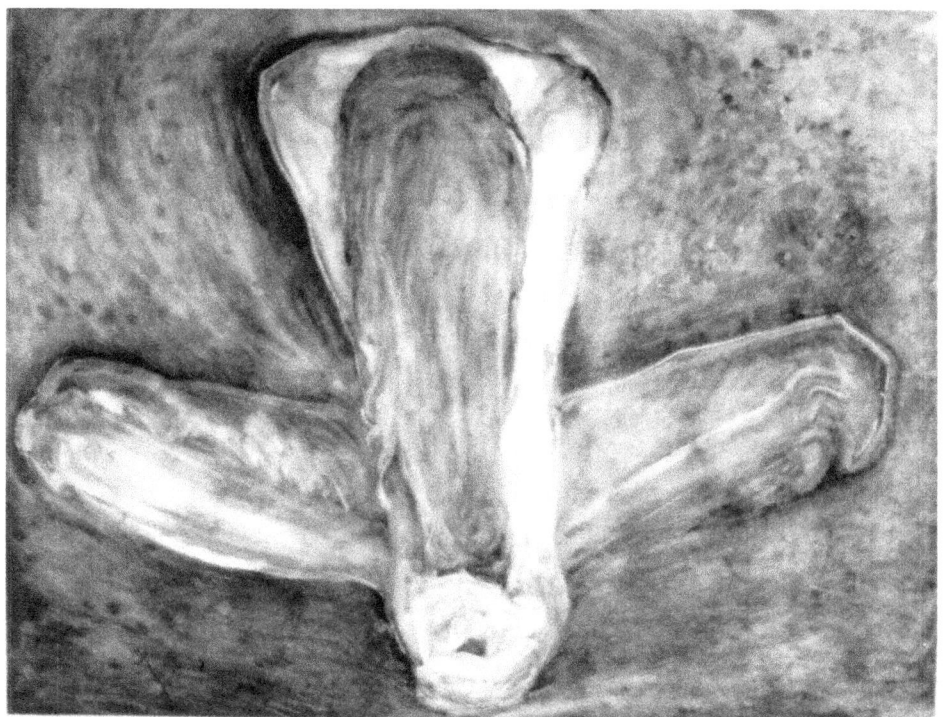

Fig. 32 Irene Vincent, *Butterfly Woman*, 1985, monotype: oil on archival paper, 18"H x 24"W

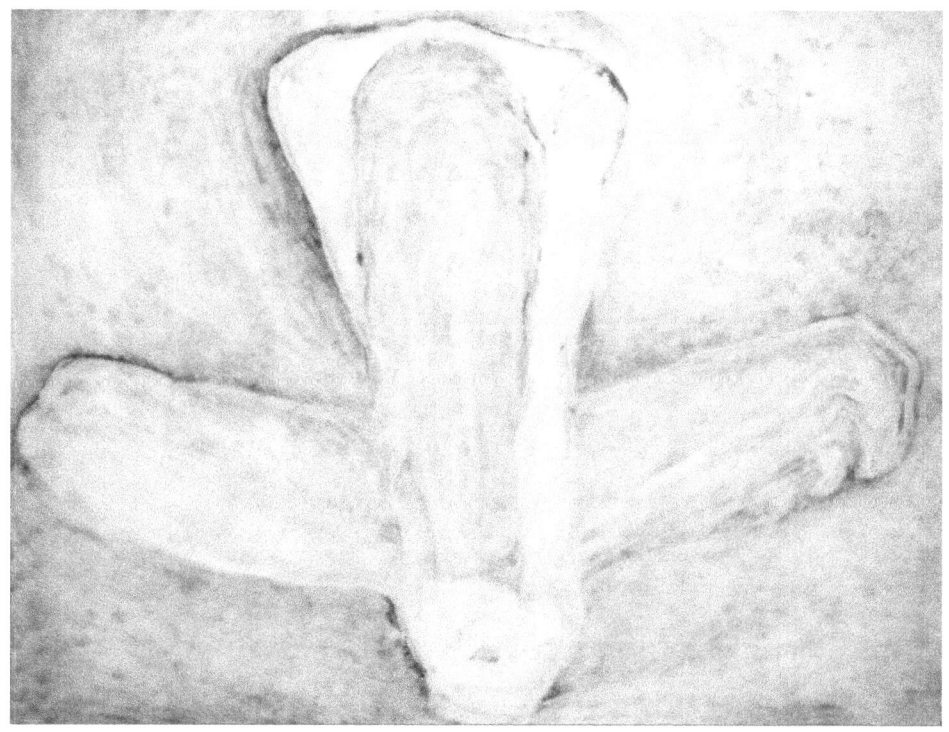

Fig. 33 Irene Vincent, *Inner Spaces*, 1985, monotype: oil on archival paper (ghost print) Sold

AWAKENING LOVE'S VIBRATIONS

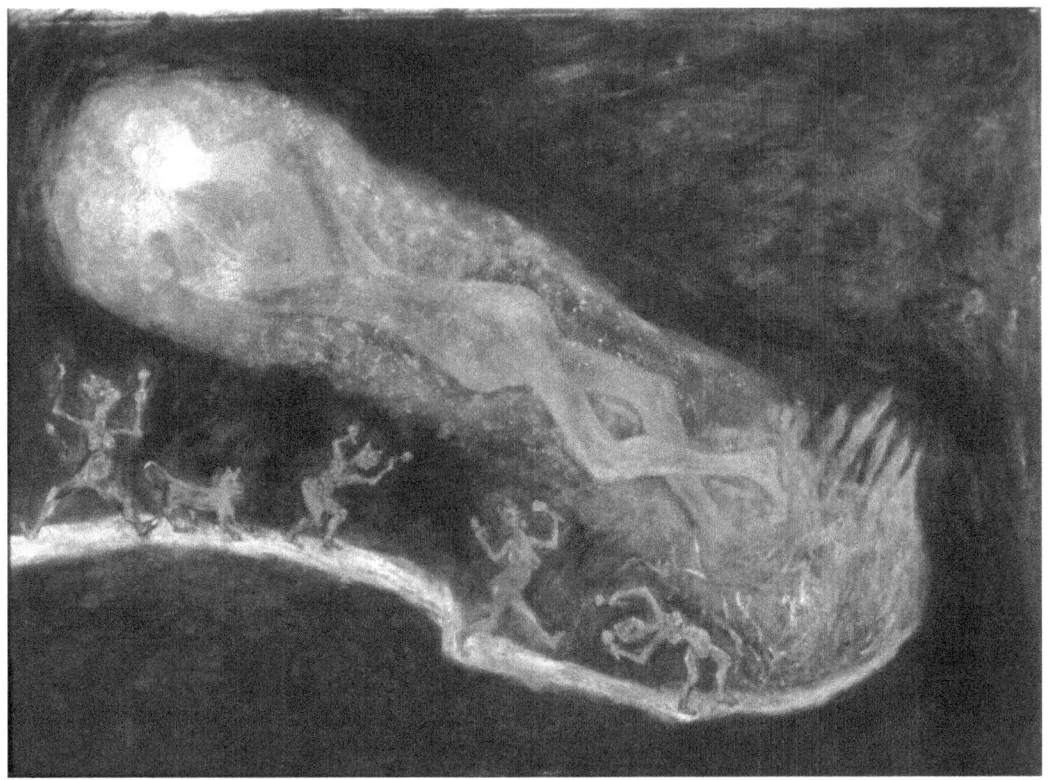

Fig. 34 Irene Vincent, *Shamanic Journey – Transmutation*, 1984, monotype: oil on archival paper, 18H" x 24W"

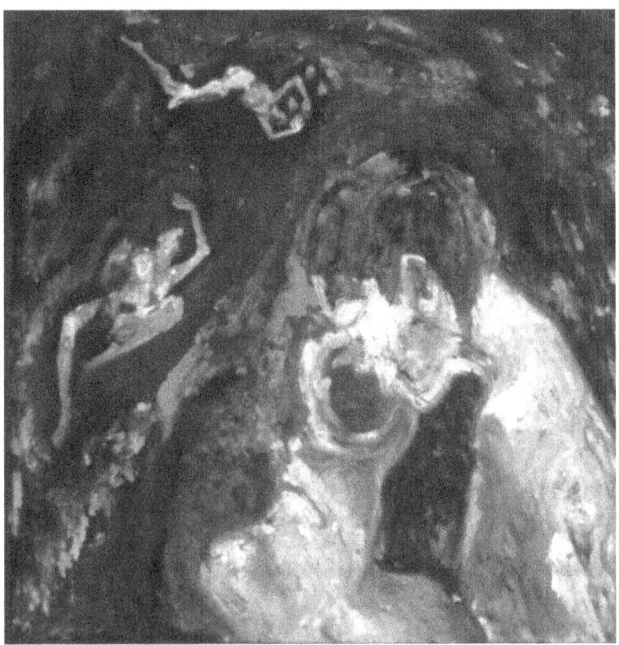

Fig. 35 Irene Vincent, *The Kiss*, 1985, monotype: oil on archival paper, 18"H x 18"H

CHAPTER FOURTEEN

Orange County Center for Contemporary Art

BECAUSE I WORKED SO MANY HOURS in my jewelry store, in my free time, I only wanted to paint, draw, and enhance my awareness. I couldn't face anything else connected to money and business. However, it seemed time to exhibit my art again. My art school friend Alexandria Allen, and I decided to join an innovative co-op gallery called Orange County Center for Contemporary Art (OCCCA), organized by Valerie Bechtol. Valerie had previously been my performance art teacher at Laguna Beach School of Art. From hand-made paper, she made large works of politically-oriented art.

She was good at developing membership and exchange shows for us artists, and for other galleries. Once we'd been active members for eighteen months, each of us had a one-person show. OCCCA set a fire to my passion, because now I would have venues in which to show my art. At OCCCA, I served on the Exhibitions Committee from 1985 to 1987.

One of our best exchange shows was with the Amos Eno Gallery in New York City. Upon arriving at the La Guardia Airport in NYC, Alexandria and I waited for our luggage to emerge on the conveyor belt. Someone's suitcase had broken open, spilling underwear and other clothes on the conveyor belt, toppling on the dirty floor.

Alexandria said, "Oh look at that, some schmuck's stuff is falling all over the place. You would think they'd buy a new suitcase."

Stunned, I whispered, "Alexandria, show a little compassion. That's so embarrassing."

Suddenly, she screamed and ran frantically toward the conveyer belt. "Oh shit, those are *my* clothes all over the place. I'm the poor schmuck."

I thought that she was joking with me, but she wasn't. We laughed, chasing and gathering up her clothes. The other passengers laughed along with us.

A *So Ho* newspaper, "Art Speak," did a favorable critique of our group show. they printed an image of my *Bird Man Meets Cat Woman* monotype (see Fig 36). We had fun partying with some of the New York artists, traveling around to as many of the galleries and art museums as we could fit into our agenda.

Together, Alexandria and I traveled around the city. She was very avant-garde, which made her exponentially fun. She wore a vest covered with painted plastic frogs. When a person commented on

AWAKENING LOVE'S VIBRATIONS

her vest, she would point to a frog near her heart, and say, "He squeaks because he was my prince. I kissed him and turned him into a frog."

Alexandria and I took a subway to the Cathedral of Saint John. We marveled at the famous stained glass Rose Window. I'd read that the window's image looked similar to a cross section of our DNA, as seen through the lens of an electron microscope. This provoked so many questions in me. Did the ancient monks, seers, and shamans have visions of these universal symbols in their meditations? Do most symbols originate in the coding of our DNA in order to guide our spirits? Did sacred geometry arise from men observing the stars? Is the sacred geometry in our DNA part of the holographic geometry of the universe?

The political sculptures and paintings protesting war and other subjects in the cathedral made a huge impression upon me. I thought, *Wow, what an innovative church.* A priest, in seeing my amazement told me that the Native Americans held special ceremonies in the cathedral. He gave us a guided tour of some of the art pieces.

Alexandria and I had a great trip together. It forged us a lifelong friendship. We also shared an interest in Jungian psychology and astrology, looking at our personal astrological charts, talking about our lives and art.

In *Bird Man Meets Cat Woman*, the figures are dancing in the sky. Cat Woman is twirling energy in her hands. Bird Man's wings are wrapped around himself either for protection or to become more of a projectile. Bird Man is looking up to the sky for answers.

Fig. 36 Irene Vincent, *Bird Man Meets Cat Woman*, 1985, monotype: oil on archival paper, 24"H x18"W

CHAPTER FIFTEEN

Missile Totem of the Ejecting Heart Transforms Itself

O NE OF THE GREAT ATTRIBUTES of my new neighborhood was the Irvine Art Center. I signed up for a clay sculpture class that offered open studio days and firing of the clay pieces. Julia Klimek, the ceramics teacher, gave us the technical knowledge necessary to complete our visions. Julia had sculpted unique clay benches for the City of Laguna Beach. You can still see one of them on Pacific Coast High Way across from the Laguna Beach Museum of Art.

At first, I made a few unique practical items: a book-reading holder for my large art books and a few magazine holders that looked like metamorphic animals. While using a stick to make drumming sounds and rhythms, I beat various textures into the clay. The special sculpture clay allowed me to make thick-edged objects that wouldn't crack in the heat of the kiln. Feeling somewhat proficient in the medium, I decided to work on a large project.

Still obsessed with the destructive capacity of the missile, I started hand-building a clay, missile-man totem. He was going to be six feet tall, with a big hole in his chest area to symbolize modern man's emptiness. I was going to design a heart for him that felt very organic, such as a thick gel-filled balloon that would be hooked to an electrical tube which in turn would be hooked to a clock set on a geometrical time progression. The concept was that the heart would eject at set time intervals and the spectator would have to replace the heart back into the missile man's chest cavity. The more times people put his heart back in place, the longer it would stay. After a certain amount of people participated, the missile would retain his heart and symbolically would no longer have a desire to kill others. This was meant to get people thinking about their own hearts, to feel responsibility and empowerment towards their own future.

After a few consecutive days of work, my clay missile was almost finished, standing at four feet high. *Just one more day of work and I'll be finished with this part, and then it can dry for the firing*, I thought. I put a few moist towels on it and covered it in plastic to keep the clay workable. This helped it to dry very slow in order to prevent cracks. But for the next few days I had to refocus and get back to work at the jewelry store. Time passed slowly for that part of my life.

The next time I walked into the clay studio, a few artists stared at me. John ran over to me, gently grabbed my arm and blocked me from going to my sculpture.

As Shirley watched, John said, "Irene your sculpture might be destroyed. It got too wet from the damp towels and it collapsed. It happens … we didn't want you to go in there…without knowing this."

"Well, how bad is it?" I asked. My stomach felt queasy. "Maybe I could retrieve it."

I started to think that perhaps this was a sign from the universe saying that I had contemplated missiles long enough. Apprehensively, I pulled the damp towels off the collapsed clay sculpture.

Astonished, I said, "It looks like something in between a human torso and a fish … like a mermaid."

My face beamed with immense joy at the sight of its beauty. In my mind's eye, I could see its completed form.

Looking perplexed, John said, "We thought you were going to cry. Some people go on a rampage when their clay sculptures collapse or crack in the kiln."

"Actually, I was tired of thinking about the missile crisis. I can see this piece as a finished sculpture." With enthusiasm, I continued, "I might be able to finish it today. Can you help me put the clay on a longer wood board for support?"

In unison, they said, "Sure we'll help you."

I gently beat the thick clay with the corners of my square stick, forming triangular marks, making some deeper and larger and some smaller to create a sense of fish scales and movement. Along the edges of the mermaid's fins, I used the long edge of the stick to form lines of angled textures. I cut away a few pieces of clay. After working on the clay sculpture for five hours, I brought its form to completion. The sculpture dried slowly for a few weeks and then was fired, but without glazes. It's difficult to control the colors of glazes, and I knew how I wanted to color the mermaid.

A few days later, I painted the sculpture with acrylic paint. The first coat was red to give it passion and life. Using a dry brush loaded with orange paint, I brushed orange over the fins. On the raised surface, I used bluish-green colors to symbolize the primordial ocean, emotions, and the collective consciousness. I named her *Molting of the Mermaid* (see Fig. 37*)*. I felt the missile had transformed itself, similar to a snake shedding its skin, being renewed. The missile had turned itself into an abstract woman fish, a mermaid.

Besides holding art classes, The Irvine Art Center offered a great gallery space for art exhibits. They offered Irvine artists a show upon juried approval in the gallery's Portfolio section. I submitted my portfolio and they gave me a show in July 1986. I exhibited several monotypes and *Molting of the Mermaid*. In the Entertainment/Arts section of the Irvine World News, Miki G. Hammond included a picture of my monotype, *Shaman Dream Dance* (see Fig. 27) and wrote: … "the works possess a cosmic, mystical quality inherent in the private evolution of an artist."

Fig. 37 Irene Vincent, Back view of *Molting of the Mermaid*, 1986, Acrylic painted over clay sculpture

Fig. 38 Irene Vincent, Side view of *Molting of the Mermaid*, 1986, sculpture, 14"H x 19"W x 28"L

AWAKENING LOVE'S VIBRATIONS

Fig. 39 Julie, Irene, and Brenda are attending Irene's exhibit, Irvine Art center, 1986

Fig. 40 Left - I. Vincent, Sketch of *Missile Totem of the Ejecting Heart*
Fig. 41 Right - I. Vincent, Sketch of *The Universe and Misguided Missiles*

CHAPTER SIXTEEN

Meeting Swami Vishnudevanand of Allahabad, India

IN 1986, AFTER SPONSORING some of Swami Shantanand's lectures in my home, he asked if his guru from Allahabad, India might visit for a few weeks. I happily accepted the offer. Swami Vishnudevanand was eighty-seven years young and gave some riveting and inspiring lectures. He would become so enthused when speaking that he would sometimes go on for three hours.

One day, I gently said, "Swami, people seem to get tired when your lectures go on for so long. Is there a way you could just speak for an hour and a half?"

"Oh, Irene," he said in his heavy Indian accent, "sometimes people don't listen right away, and when I see that they're engaged, the words for them keep coming. I become more energized when I see that they're being inspired."

I could see that there was nothing more to say to Swami about that matter. At his age, Swami Vishnudevanand was very disciplined and wanted me to know his routine.

Swami said, "I get up at five in the morning, I clean myself, stand on my head for an hour and do a few yoga asanas. My teacher used to find two branches close together in a tree and hang upside down for two hours. The headstand is king of the asanas and makes your mind strong. It heals almost every ailment that the body can have, including mental disturbances. Did you know that if people did the headstand that there would be no tuberculosis in the world? Through the inversion asana, the lungs can cleanse themselves."

I just sat there at the breakfast table, wide eyed and with raised eyebrows, in my neophyte amazement.

Swami continued, "I go for an hour walk, I eat a bowl of vegetable curry, and I write letters to my disciples and devotees. I write in three diaries. At my age, I keep a diary of everything I eat. If my knee swells or I get an unhealthy symptom in my body, I can look at what I have eaten over the past few days or so and change my diet, in order to bring my body back to a healthy state. In the second diary, I write about my meditations, philosophical, and spiritual thoughts. In the third diary, I keep track of my daily activities. Then I meditate for a few hours, disappearing into wondrous metaphysical realms. Around five o'clock I eat my vegetable curry and rice for dinner. I just eat two meals a day. After dinner, I go for an hour walk. Students can come and walk with me, then. I like to go to sleep by eight o'clock, if I am not giving a lecture."

Guruji added, "Your teacher should have spiritual experiences, not just bookish knowledge. It's best if your teacher has experienced his teachings. Also, his words, his teachings should be one with his character. Observe and use your discrimination when listening to a teacher."

"Yes, Guruji," I said. "I've noticed that sometimes when I read spiritual or intellectual books, the author is just repeating something he has read or heard, and it hasn't affected his character or life. Sometimes when I read, there have been a few teachers where the information doesn't ring true to my heart."

"It's so wonderful that you have lived such a disciplined life," I continued. "There are many things I can learn from you. You know, Swami, there was a time in my life that I thought of discipline as a horrible word, something people of authority enforced upon me. But now I see it as self-discipline, a way to organize and enhance my life. Any time you come to America, you can stay with me for two to three weeks. I'll help your student Carlos raise funds for your airplane ticket. Then I'll set up one or two lectures for you to give in my home."

Later that morning Swami Shantanand asked me if I wanted to join him, Sushil, and Guruji to visit Yogananda's gardens in Encinitas, California. I couldn't think of a better way to spend my day off work. I called my artist friend Don Chase and asked him to go with us.

That first meeting with Swami was wonderful. I thought about how, when I was nineteen, I'd wanted to meet a wise old man. You know, the kind with the long white beard. Well, the wise elder finally showed up into my life, in multiples. I now had Swami Radha, Guruji, Swami Shantanand, Swami Sahajananda and the Dalai Lama as guiding lights. And a spiritual family of supportive friends.

I felt appreciation in my heart, looked up into the sky, and said, "Thank you, Divine Universe!"

Fig. 42 Irene praying at Yogananda's Gardens in Encinitas, CA

Fig. 43 – Left - Guruji blesses Irene at Yogananda's Gardens in Encinitas, CA.

Fig. 44 – Right - Swami Vishnudevanand Saraswati of Allahabad, India at Kuma Mela Gathering. Photography by Carlos Ballantyne.

AWAKENING LOVE'S VIBRATIONS

Fig. 45 Irene and Guruji are standing in the background. Sushil, Don, and Shantanand are in the foreground.

CHAPTER SEVENTEEN

Seeking Oneness & Oneness in Thought

OVER A PERIOD OF TIME, as part of my creative process, I would think about a concept or a particular subject. Then in a flash, the whole image would come into my mind's eye. In this way, the vision of *Seeking Oneness* was born from years of contemplating the woman's feminist movement and the concept of "true equality of the sexes".

I contemplated the feminist movement from the early 1970's to 1986. While I was happy for the newly acquired equalities, I was concerned that in order to gain power women had started dressing like men, becoming more aggressive, and copying negative male traits. Originally, I wanted to paint an image showing women taking on these negative male attributes and also to include an image showing how they could gain equality while bringing the nobler female attributes of love and creativity into mainstream society and business. Even though a lot of ideas popped into my head, I couldn't get an image that inspired me.

During 1984 to 1986, while studying dreams with a Jungian Dream Group, I gained insight into the anima and animus, the inner male and inner female. This dream-work helped me process my thoughts of equality for both the feminine and the masculine in society, in my personal relationships, and for my own inner male and female aspects.

Churning also in my mind was the grand concept of an orgasmic union with the Cosmos, and meditating on That Which is Most High, as Swami Radha had put it. In addition, Gurugi's constant waves of bliss, along with his lectures that duality is an illusion provided more contemplative food for the vision.

One morning in 1986, while sitting at my kitchen table, as I took a sip of coffee, the whole vision for *Seeking Oneness* came in a flash with a voice describing the vision. I quickly grabbed a pencil and paper and started drawing as the voice said, "The painting is to be a twelve-foot equilateral triangle divided into seven canvases, featuring an outer male and female figure, seeking the divine. Then in another panel, their souls are embracing, to be shown as more transparent and ethereal-looking figures, depicting the union of the inner male and female energies.

"In the top triangular panel, paint an image of the six-sided star with a spirit bird and its wings forming a circle around the star. The spirit bird will also be blessing the embrace of the souls in the panel below it.

AWAKENING LOVE'S VIBRATIONS

The voice continued, "Paint an image of a little red triangle with its point facing down and then put this triangle in a circle within the star to symbolize heaven blessing us. The upward pointing triangular structure of the whole canvas symbolizes our devotion to the heavens, the cosmos.

"In a square panel at the center bottom, paint footprints showing the sacred path we're all on and a snake biting its tail depicting eternity."

It was a Saturday morning and I searched around the house for Robert, finding him in the garage. I asked him to get a ladder, climb it and take some instant pictures of me lying on the floor, so I could pose like I was flying. Then I took some of him. Using a timer, we photographed us embracing.

After staring at the photos and my new little drawing, the image of the six-sided star made of two interlocking triangles perplexed me. At first, I thought it was too ethnic, representing only Judaism. However, after researching it, I found that it had origins in many cultures including Tibetan, Egyptian, and Judaism. The six-sided star symbolized the marriage of Heaven and Earth, the union of the male and female, and so forth. This star, known to many of us as the Star of David, symbolized the whole meaning of the painting.

Fig. 46 Irene Vincent, *Seeking Oneness*, 1986, acrylic on raw canvas, seven canvases bolted together, 12ft. H x 12ft. W Base.

As a study for the central merging figures in *Seeking Oneness,* I made a quick expressive drawing of the merging figures. This drawing inspired me to make a larger one.

Fig. 47 I. Vincent, quick study for *Seeking Oneness*, 1986, charcoal drawing on paper, 13"H x 8.5"W

I decided to do a life size drawing-painting combination on a two-foot by six-foot piece of paper. While working, I visualized keeping my devotional and emotional energies alive, showing the figures being drawn into the light, into infinity. As I thought about the concept of infinity, the figure eight's spiraling lines and marks of symbolic energy took form in front of and around the figures, merging the figures' faces into the light, with only their eyes visible. As I contemplated the image, I thought about those magical moments when you know and the other person knows that you both are sharing the exact same thought. It's a psychic transmission, one of those *AHA* moments, and even beyond that. This study became its own art piece, titled *Oneness in Thought*.

AWAKENING LOVE'S VIBRATIONS

Fig. 48 I. Vincent, *Oneness in Thought*, 1986, acrylic, charcoal, and gesso on paper, 64"H x 24"W

After completing *Oneness in Thought*, I was ready to tackle the task of painting *Seeking Oneness*, which inspired me towards the experience of oneness.

Irene Vincent

Fig. 49 Irene is standing with *Seeking Oneness*, acrylic on raw stretched canvas. Seven sections are bolted together forming a 12 foot. equilateral triangle.

*"When Your
Inner Male and Female Energies Unite
Instantaneously
You Become One with All That Is."*

Irene Vincent

CHAPTER EIGHTEEN

The Unexpected Trip to Thailand

IN 1986, AN LA-BASED JEWELRY importer called Thailand Products offered ten of their best wholesale customers a free trip for ten days to Thailand. I was one of the ten lucky customers invited.

"Irene, it'll be a first-class trip," said Jin. "We'll take you to Bangkok, Chiang Mai, and the southern beaches. You'll like the other people who are coming. You'll get to see our factories. We'll go this spring. Do you want to come with us?"

"Yes, of course, but can I bring my boyfriend, Robert?"

"Just pay for Robert's airplane fare. We'll pay for the rest."

"Wow. I can't wait."

The next time I went to buy jewelry, the owners, Jin and Chan said, "Irene, we want to invite you to our home in Los Angeles for dinner tonight. You'll get to experience the best Thai food at our home. After dinner, Chan will drive you back to the train station and you can catch the late train to San Juan Capistrano. Can you return to our booth at 6 PM?"

"Yes," I said, "I'd love to have dinner with you, especially in your home."

Later that night, when I walked into their home, fine aromas of exotic spices filled my nostrils. Several Thai people carried platters filled with curried noodles, vegetables, and meats, and set them atop a mahogany dining table.

Amazed, I asked, "Are you having a huge dinner party?"

Jin replied, "Every night, we have our cooks place food on our table. Our extended family members are welcomed for food every evening. Our home is open to them. Irene, you fill up your plate first. Our relatives often eat from the same dishes with their hands and it might not be appealing to you."

I filled my plate, astonished at the variety.

Upon savoring my first bite, I said, "This is so delicious. Thank you so much."

As I ate the delectable food, I was surprised at the number of relatives that kept coming to the table to fill their plates. Quite impressed by Gin and Chan's hospitality, I looked forward to going to Thailand with these kind people.

Finally, spring came and we were in Thailand. On our first day in Bangkok, we toured an ancient elaborate city temple and saw the huge golden Buddha. My fellow traveling companions stared at me, whispering and giggling, while I took time to say prayers and light incense. I felt judged, but I didn't care. As we took a tour bus ride around the city, I saw people stop and pray at spiritual shrines along the edges of the streets. It was my first encounter with an openly spiritual culture, one that didn't encourage spirituality's restriction to temples, synagogues, churches and mosques, and it filled my heart with a joy.

Then we toured their jewelry factory. The jewelers were paid only $1.00 per hour, but they were given three fresh cooked meals per day, clean apartments, and health care. The workers appeared relatively happy, and they looked healthy. They were eating real food verses the processed junk food so many Americans eat.

That evening in the hotel, we had an incident. I had brought along a foot massager, which I'd bought to alleviate the pain from spending long hours on my feet in my jewelry store. The foot massager took away a lot of the pain. With all the touring, I figured I could comfort my feet. I also brought the electric transformers and plugs for Thailand. However, when I plugged the massager into the transformer and into the wall socket, sparks flew and everything suddenly went dark.

"Robert help!" I cried. "This thing has caught on fire."

"Throw a towel on it and pull the plug," he yelled back.

"It's melted. The plastic fumes are horrible. I'm scared of being electrocuted."

Through the darkness, Robert made his way to the bathroom and pulled the plug. "Do you think we should call the front desk?"

Ignoring his question, I said, "Oh shit, I hear sirens and people running around. Robert, stick your head out in the hallway and see what is happening. I am so embarrassed."

As Robert opened the door, a hotel attendant was running by and said, "All the electricity on this floor has gone out. I'm sure it's just a fuse. We'll have it fixed shortly."

"Irene, should we let them know that you caused this?"

"Are you serious? The wall plug seems okay. Nothing is smoking. I'd just as soon not tell them. They might charge us or throw us out of here. Let's get rid of the evidence."

Robert started laughing, spilling out his words, "This could make for some pretty funny stories. Irene melted her massager."

I burst out laughing and could barely say, "Don't you dare say a word, at least not until near the end of our trip. They'll all tease me."

"I'll give it a few days."

Thank God it didn't take long for the lights to turn back on. When we saw the time, we scurried down to meet every one for dinner. During that first dinner, waiter after waiter kept bringing us different meat and vegetable dishes whiffing of aromatic spices. It was amazing and comical at the same time. Just as we thought the meal was through a new dish of food would appear. I couldn't imagine how we were to eat all this food. The meal was a feast, just like at Jin's home.

The next day we rode an overnight train to Chiang Mai located in northern Thailand. Close to 11 PM, at one of the stops, the train filled with tenacious mosquitoes. My natural repellant didn't deter these hungry pests. Gin and Chan were ready with their special sprays. After a few minutes of high anxiety, all was quiet again.

The next morning, we continued our tour, tired from lack of sleep. We visited multicolored poppy fields, the vista filled with their beauty. Nearby was a Tibetan refugee village, where I bought some Buddha Tankas, sacred images painted on cloth. In the afternoon, we went to an ancient Tibetan monastery located up hundreds of stairs. As with the Mayan ruins at Chichen Itza, there were sculptured snake guardians undulating along the sides of the stairs, their heads rearing up at the bottom. Over the snake's heart was a diamond-shaped mandala. It was interesting how sacred sites around the world bore so many similar images and symbols.

After a few days, we headed to southern Thailand to see the beautiful beaches. Then it was back home to California.

Fig. 50 Jim, Robert and Irene are standing in front of the Golden Buddha in Thailand.

Fig. 51 Our tour group in Thailand

Fig. 52 Left - Elephant ride in northern Thailand
Fig. 53 Right - View of the snake guardians and monks coming down the stairs.

Fig. 54 Left – Irene is standing near a Tibetan refugee village's gate.
Fig. 55 Right - Irene is in a Poppy field

Fig. 56 Irene is standing next to a snake guardian at the steps below the Tibetan temple.

CHAPTER NINETEEN

Good News, Bad News, What's the Difference?

ONCE HOME, I FOCUSED ON business and completing artwork for my solo exhibit at OCCCA in January 1987. The huge gallery space was divided into three large sections. For solo shows, we always had another member in the second gallery and an invited artist in the third gallery. Time passed quickly.

The exhibit had a large turnout and received nice reviews. In the review from Art Scene, January 1987, titled 'Gilah Yelin Hirsh, Michael Wingo, & Irene Vincent', Kathy Zimmerer wrote the following about my work, "Vincent employs primal images in monotypes and paintings to create startling effects. In 'Journey of the Soul', a figure curled up like a fetus floats in swirling limbo between birth and death, day and night. In 'Echoes of Devotion', a genie emerges from the whirling ground to give a haunting cry. The magical ambience of 'Echoes' is intensified by the scumbled surfaces and the dissolving forms. Other strong works include the nightmarish 'Bird Man Meets Cat Woman' #1, in which Vincent pinpoints our archetypal fear of the metamorphosis from man into beast." It was interesting for me to see her point of view.

When it was my time to work at the desk for OCCCA, another artist said to me, "Oh, Irene, did Julie tell you that an assistant curator from the LA art museum really liked your work?"

"No, no one has told me anything. Did she get his name or his business card for me?"

"No, she told him to take one of your postcards."

"Did she say which LA Art Museum he is associated with?"

"No, she never asked."

"How am I supposed to find him?"

"I don't know. Call the curators in both museums."

I sat there upset, thinking, *I just spent all this money to show and promote my art, and now an opportunity is gone, either out of the other artist's indifference, laziness, or sabotage.*

I had made plans to find the curator and figure out what to say to him. However, an employee quit, and suddenly Ron and I had to cover their work load, and then help our manager to hire and train a new person. At times work seemed endless. A few months went by and then I remembered that I hadn't tried to call and I lost my nerve. I would get times when I felt confident about promoting myself, but when work at the store took away my spare time I would question how will I manage to paint enough to be taken seriously and keep the business running.

Feeling hurt from the missed opportunity, I thought about quitting OCCCA when my contract ended towards the end of 1987. Like many artists, I was upset I had to pay to show my work so that the public could be entertained. At least my jewelry business rewarded me with a good income.

Continuing to paint on my days off, I'd decided to semi-drop out of the art scene. I chose to travel to more sacred sites and pursue my spiritual path more diligently. Art was an important part of my path, but there were many other adventures ahead of me.

The next time Swami Sahajananda came to visit, he asked, "How did your art exhibit go?"

"Overall, it went well," I said, feeling a pain in the pit of my stomach.

He saw the disappointment in my face as I told him my story.

Swami said, "Irene, do you know the ancient Chinese story, "Good News, Bad News, What's the Difference?"

"No Swami, I haven't. I could use a story right now."

Swami's face lit up with a wide smile. He said, "A farmer had a beautiful mare and just before planting season, she ran off. The neighbors came and said to the farmer, 'Oh, we feel so sorry for you. It'll soon be time to plough your fields and you don't have a horse. How will you manage?'

"The farmer said, 'Good news, bad news, what's the difference?'

"Shortly thereafter, the mare came back with a fine stud in tow. That day all the neighbors came to admire the farmer's new horse.

"They said, 'You're so lucky, you now have two horses.'

"The farmer said, 'Good news, bad news, what's the difference?'

"While the farmer's son was training the new wild horse, the horse threw him to the ground and broke his leg.

"The neighbors came and said, 'You, poor man. We feel so sorry for you. Your son is disabled. How will you be able to harvest your crops when it's time?'

"The farmer shook his head, raised his eyebrows, and replied, 'Good news, bad news, what's the difference?'

"Shortly thereafter, a war broke out somewhere in the country, the army passed through the village taking all the able-bodied youths as soldiers, except they didn't take the man's son because his leg was broken.

"The neighbors came and said to the farmer, 'You're so lucky, you still have your son. If he heals in time, he can help you harvest.'

"The farmer replied, 'Good news, bad news, what's the difference?'

"Then it turned out that the farmer's mare was pregnant, and so gave birth to two colts. Of course, the neighbors all came to celebrate and tell the farmer, 'You're so lucky.'

"And he replied, 'Good news, bad news, what's the difference?'"

"Thanks Swami. This story is one of the most comforting stories I've ever heard. Now I realize that there's no reason to lose my center of peace over elation or sadness. Why judge circumstances when they transform themselves? Every day is a new day."

"Irene, I hope that you'll continue painting. Don't let this incident discourage you."

"I have to paint, Swami. It's my self-expression. I get a deeper understanding of myself and my soul from contemplating the images of my visions and dreams. However, I only have so much time. I figure I just won't show my art for a while. Though the wonderful thing about the show was that it focused my energy because of the deadline. Finishing so many art pieces made me happy."

"I think that you've made a wise choice," Swami replied. "At some point in time, you'll want to show your art again."

"I'm sure I will," I said.

Then, after a few seconds of sweet silence, I said, "Swami Vishnudevanand gave a lecture with a similar concept. He said, 'Day follows night, night follows day. Everything goes in cycles. Everything is always changing. You can always count on change in this outer world. The one thing, only, that is unchanging, is your inner most indwelling spirit.' I really loved this story, 'Good News, Bad News – What's the Difference?' I'll have to remember it."

❖ ❖ ❖

Fig. 57, Fig. 58, & Fig. 59 Vincent, *Mayan Venus/Cat Goddess Singing to the Stars*, 1987, clay sculpture, 13.5"H x 8"W x 6"L

AWAKENING LOVE'S VIBRATIONS

Fig. 60, Fig. 61, and Fig. 62 I. Vincent, *Mayan-Spiral Venus*, 1987, clay sculpture, 10"H x 5"W x 5L"

CHAPTER TWENTY

Mayan Goddess Sculptures

AFTER MY SOLO SHOW with OCCCA, we did an exchange art exhibit with Spectrum Gallery in San Diego where I showed my sculpture, *Cat Man Pushing Back Illusions of Darkness*. After this show, my OCCCA membership expired. It was hard separating from the group at OCCCA. However, the Irvine Art Center became my new place to make artist friends.

I felt the universe was guiding me to give more of my energy to spiritual, mythological, and shamanic contemplations. At the Irvine Art Center, I proceeded to make a series of Mayan Goddess sculptures that were 8 inches to 14 inches tall. I hand-shaped the clay and then beat it with a small stick into forms resembling an ancient Goddess, or something that spoke to my psyche. After pondering over pages of Mayan symbols, I proceeded to carve them into my work. One of my favorite sculptures became *Venus/Cat Goddess Singing to the Stars*.

From this process, I was seeking to gain ancient wisdom from the Mayan culture and to further understand the meanings of their symbols. As I researched symbols that appeared in my art and dreams, I found that these same symbols appeared in numerous ancient cultures, and even held similar meaning across those cultures. It was becoming clear to me that the symbol's inherent meanings invoked the mysteries of the universe.

Another favorite little sculpture of mine was *Star Being*, who looked like a wispy ghost or an ET. I engraved a spiral over his main body to symbolize primordial energy, as well as the Milky Way. A diamond shape carved at his throat showed him voicing higher wisdom, and a grooved circle with a dot in its center placed inside the diamond shape depicted Star Being's inherent balance. The back of *Star Being* looked like a cobra, which represents kundalini energy or wisdom.

AWAKENING LOVE'S VIBRATIONS

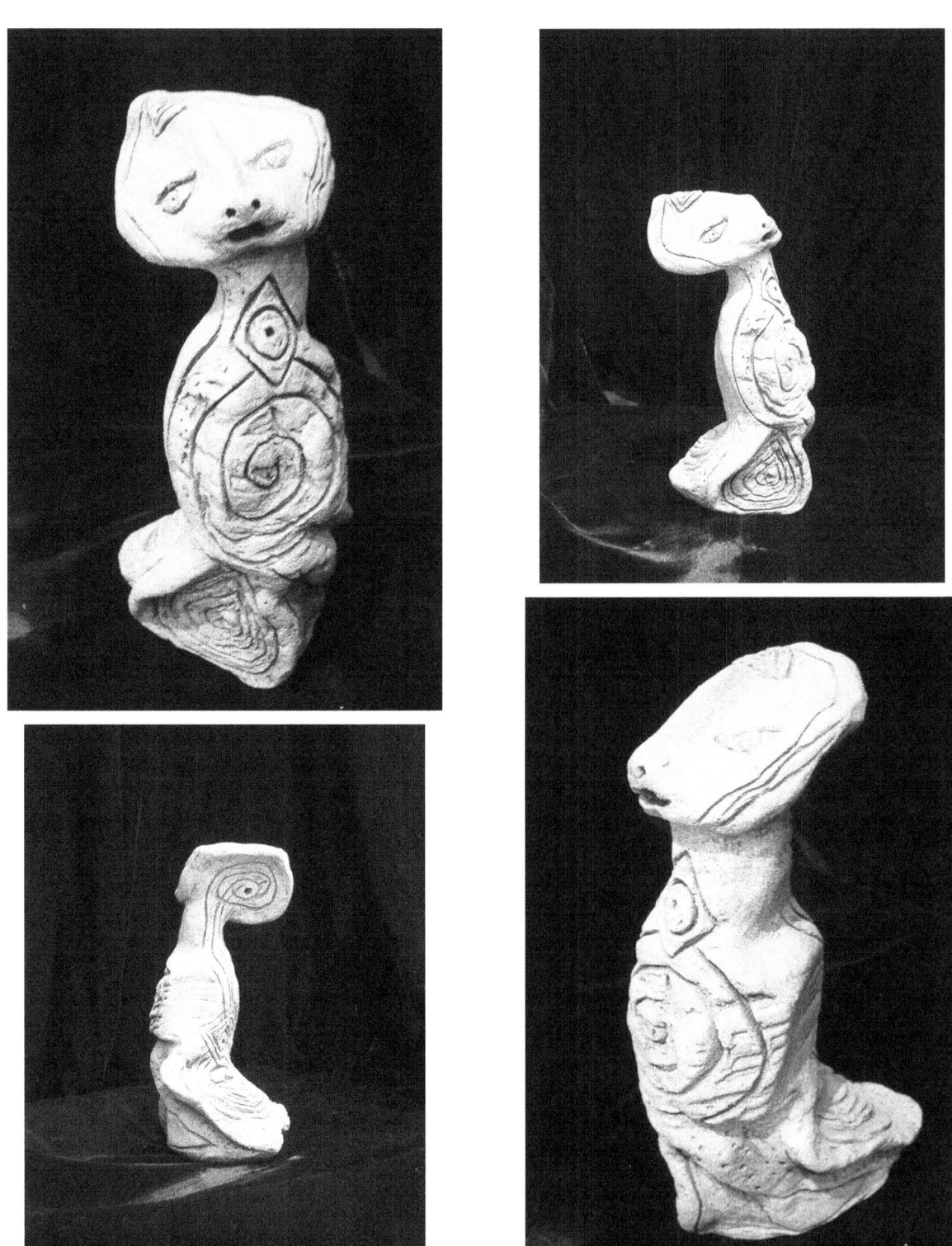

Fig. 63, Fig. 64, Fig. 65, & Fig. 66 Irene Vincent, views of *Star Being*, 1987, clay sculpture, 9"H x 3.5"W x 4.5"L

CHAPTER TWENTY-ONE

Mayan Ruins: Tikal, Guatemala

FINALLY, THE DAY CAME for Robert and I to travel to Guatemala. Robert and I usually traveled with a loose plan of knowing what sites we wanted to visit in a given country, since we believed we got better rates on tours and rooms once we were there. And we usually carried a Frommer's travel book. Learning from past experience, we booked at least the first night's lodging.

Our first hotel in Guatemala City had a lovely old colonial lobby that in its heyday must have been luxurious. A young man assisted us and carried our luggage up to our room. He opened our room door revealing a huge suite that, while clean, had a vaguely worn, aged look. We were nonetheless amazed.

After the attendant left, Robert said, "Are you sure they didn't make a mistake? If this room cost seventy dollars, maybe we can get a less expensive room. We still have another day here."

"Okay, when we go down for dinner, let's ask for another room."

We relaxed for an hour, then proceeded down the elevator to the front desk. I asked the man if they had any cheaper rooms available.

The clerk said, "No, we don't have any more rooms."

Robert and I then proceeded to the concierge to figure out how we would get to Tikal, the most magnificent of the Mayan ruins.

As we approached the concierge sitting at a lone desk in a hallway, Robert asked, "Do you speak English?"

The concierge said, "Yes."

I said, "Can you please tell us the best way to travel to Tikal, so we can see the Mayan ruins? We want to stay there for a few nights. And we'd like to leave tomorrow morning."

Her face grimaced. With a hint of sadness, she said, "There is a twin-engine plane in two days, but it's booked. You have to take a plane to a town near the site, and then a bus ride."

"Going to Tikal is why I came here," I said. "Is there a bus? Or can we check somewhere else?"

"I can put you on a waiting list. Sometimes people cancel their trips." Hesitating, she continued, "Especially after today."

"What do you mean?"

"Our single engine tour plane crashed in the jungle today. The jungle swallows up planes. It may never be found. That's why it is better that you fly in a twin-engine plane. If one engine dies, you still have a chance. Do you still want to be on the waiting list?"

Robert and I looked at each other, digesting this bit of bad news.

I replied, "Yes, I really want to go to Tikal. It's very important to me. And when we go, will you be able to book us a room in a hotel at the ruins?"

"Yes, but only for one night. Come see me tomorrow afternoon."

As Robert and I headed to the dining room, I said, "Well, that was a bit depressing. Maybe when we walk around town tomorrow, we'll see someone else offering tours."

"We'll figure it out," Robert replied. Let's eat and rest."

The next morning, while eating breakfast in the hotel restaurant, we noticed an American-looking couple at a nearby table. We smiled at them.

The casually dressed man said, "Hi, did you just arrive?"

Robert replied, "Yes, last night."

Waving his arm open from his chair, acting as if he owned the place, he said, "Welcome, my name is Jim and my wife's name is Sue. We've been here for three months now."

I asked "How are you liking your stay?"

Jim grinned. "It's a great room for twenty dollars."

Surprised, I exclaimed, "Twenty dollars? We're paying seventy. We tried to get a cheaper room, but they didn't have any more."

"Oh, the government won't let the hotel change your initial rate when you book from out of the country. You have to pack up your luggage, pay your bill, walk out the door and then come back in and ask for a room."

"Are you kidding me?"

Sue chimed in, "You'll probably get your same room for twenty dollars. Go get your bags now. It'll save you some money."

They proceeded to tell us about the former day's plane crash, and the ensuing search efforts.

"Yes, the concierge told us about the plane crash," I said. "I'm still hoping to go to Tikal."

"It's truly a magnificent site," Jim said. "We went there last year."

"Well, it was nice meeting you. We had better get going."

"See you around the lobby," they chimed.

Robert and I were apprehensive about giving up our room, but the thought of saving money egged us on. We went downstairs, checked out, walked out the door, and came back into the lobby.

Feeling embarrassed, I said, "Senor, do you have an inexpensive room available?"

He smiled, knowing the game, "Yes, I've a room for twenty dollars. How many nights will you be staying?"

"One to two nights, we're not sure. Can we let you know tomorrow morning?"

The man replied, "Yes. Here is your key."

He gave us the same room. Robert and I were happy with our triumph. We put our luggage back, then went to explore the city. Other than a colorful market, there was a feeling of bleakness and depression. The sun was hot, reflecting heat off the surrounding cement buildings and sidewalks. Dirt flew into our eyes from the passing vehicles, exhaust fuming up our nostrils.

Upset, I looked at Robert. "I really need to get to nature. I sure hope we go to Tikal tomorrow morning. We better book a tour now for that lake you want to visit."

"I really don't like this either," said Robert.

After lunch, we found the concierge at her desk. As she looked up, she said, "I've good news. A few more tourists wanted to go to Tikal, so we hired another twin-engine airplane. Be here at 8:45 AM for the plane. It lands in Flores. Then you take a two-hour bus ride to the ruins. And I was able to get you a hotel room."

Excitement raced through my body. I could feel my insides dancing and my eyes lighting up. "Thanks so much, I said. "Here is the money. We'd also like to book a tour to some other sites in Guatemala for the next morning, after we get back."

Robert and I planned out the next six days.

There were about eight of us on the small airplane. Once we left Guatemala City, a vast jungle sprawled below us. I could see it swallowing a plane. It was beautiful. There was something about the vastness of the ocean, the sky, and the jungle that made my heart expand with love. I felt so much love for the beauty below our airplane that I felt safe. It was a bumpy ride, but with a good landing.

Once out of the airplane, we piled into a small bus. During the ride, I noticed just how much the jungle encroached the edges of the road. Now I understood how difficult it must be to keep the roads clear of vegetation.

Once we arrived, we got our room and immediately signed up for the last jungle trek of the day. The tour guide, Maria gave us a brief history along the way. Tikal's first monuments dated back to 2000 BC, and it became one of the most powerful kingdoms in ancient Maya, reaching peak dominance from about 200 AD to 900 AD. It had no rivers or nearby lakes for drinking water, so they collected their water in reservoirs.

Most of its history is known from imagery and hieroglyphs carved on its many altars, lintels, stelae (carved tablets), tombs and pyramids. She pointed to Temple IV and said, "That one is 230 feet high, the tallest pre-Columbian structure in the Americas. Make sure you have a bottle of water on you when you climb that one."

We trekked a short way from the ruins and into the luscious, overgrown exotic plants and vine-covered trees. A part of me felt scared in the jungle, not knowing its creatures. And yet, at the same time, the beauty of the well-rooted trees and the canopy of green light above created a feeling of being connected to earth and heaven. I felt loved and secure.

We climbed the stairs of an ancient pyramid long since covered by tree roots. There was a magical quality to all of this, of something long hidden and about to be revealed.

After the trek, the sun was still up, so we ran up and down the pyramids until our legs couldn't take us any farther. We rose early in the morning to explore the ruins before our 3:30 PM bus ride back to the plane. I wished that we could've stayed longer.

After spending the night back in Guatemala City, we took a bus tour to Antigua, an old Spanish colonial village. Then we traveled through the mountains, passing the Mayan villages on our way to Lake Atitlan. The beautiful lake, back dropped by mountains engendered a deep sense of serenity. *Yeah, I am out of the city.* Seeing in this natural landscape the native people dressed in their colorful clothing opened my heart, and enlivened my soul.

AWAKENING LOVE'S VIBRATIONS

Fig. 67 Vastness of the ruins and jungle at Tikal, Guatemala.

Fig. 68 Irene reflecting upon the ancient pyramid stairs covered in overgrown roots.

Fig. 69 Irene and Robert are at the ruins in Tikal, Guatemala.

Fig. 70 View of the Mayan pyramids at Tikal, Guatemala

Fig. 71 After the climb, Robert is relaxing and enjoying the view of Tikal.

Fig. 72 - Left - Colorful Guatemalan girls walking near Lake Atitlan.
Fig. 73 - Right - Lake Atitlan

CHAPTER TWENTY-TWO

The Shaman Healing Dream

THE DAY AFTER RETURNING to the USA, I fell ill with a debilitating flu. Even my business partner told me to go home and get better as quickly as possible. After three weeks of suffering and difficulty breathing, I had reached the end of my rope.

That evening, as I started to fall asleep, I said, "God, just let me die, I surrender."

That sentiment invoked a dream. I dreamt I was in the sky, a thousand feet in the air. I was standing on a disk supported by a pole. When I looked down, I became scared and at the same time, I was in awe of the beautiful red rocks of the desert looming far below me. Across from me on another disk, supported by a pole, was an old shaman man. He held out his hand for me to touch. I hesitated.

Beaming with a sweet expression on his wise, ancient face, he said, "Do you think that I would let you die? Trust me."

So, I gently reached for his hand. As our hands touched, we were suddenly down on the desert floor sitting in a circle of shamans. One shaman held out a peace pipe to me. As I looked around, I realized they were all men. I was worried I may have invaded their dreamtime.

Knowing my thoughts, the old shaman said, "Irene, you're one of us. You're supposed to be here."

With tears of remembrance, I smiled and took the peace pipe from the shaman and smoked it.

Upon awakening, I felt a vibration of bliss and happiness. I was healed. I could breath, my mind felt clear and my body was energized. The image of the shaman from the dream was so vivid. Excitedly, I searched a bookshelf for a book about shamans I had bought a while before. *Shaman: The Wounded Healer* by Joan Halifax gleamed out. His picture was on the cover. The book mentioned that Matsúwa had come to the United States to speak to members of the United Nations about taking care of Mother Earth. He was from the Huichol tribe. All the members of that tribe were welcome to become a shaman, in that, for a set period of time, they created sacred prayer art. It was a tribe where all members shared sacred equality. I remembered in the dream how welcome I was in that circle with male shamans. As I had traveled through Guatemala, I had felt such deep love for Mother Earth and for the indigenous people, praying for the continuing of their traditions. Somehow these deep feelings had drawn this wonderful shaman into my dream, or me into his.

I knew that I'd have to make a painting of this dream. However, at the moment, I had a lot of work to do at the jewelry store because of all the sick time I'd taken.

AWAKENING LOVE'S VIBRATIONS

Fig. 74 I. Vincent, *Planetary Alignment for Dream Time*, 2003, 4'H x 3'W, oil paint over acrylic on canvas.

Years later, I finished this painting after another healing dream inspired me to paint a combination of the two dreams.

CHAPTER TWENTY-THREE

Adventures in Peru and Bolivia

IN 1987, ON OUR NEXT VACATION, Robert and I flew to Lima to see the capital of Peru. Lima is an old Spanish colonial city that, for me, had a feeling of poverty and suppression. I could taste the dust lingering in the dry air. We stayed for two days and were happy to leave.

Next, we flew to Cusco, located in the center of Peru at an elevation of 11,200 feet. Cusco was the capital of the Incan Empire from the 1300's to 1532, when the Spanish arrived.

Once we made it to our hotel in Cusco, we were told to rest and drink some coca tea to help acclimate us. Our hotel room was one of many ancient stone rooms forming a rectangle with a small flowering courtyard in its center, its only redeeming feature. The room had one small narrow window and a heavy wooden door. Upon entering the room, toxic fumes burnt my nostrils, sucking the oxygen out of my lungs.

"Did they just spray for bugs or use some strong cleaning fluid?" I asked. "I can't breathe in here. I'm so tired."

Robert coughed. "It looks like the only way we're going to get a cross current in here is to leave the door open."

"I don't feel safe napping with the door open. Robert, can you go see if there is a better room with more windows?"

"Sure. Here's the can of oxygen I brought for us. Take a whiff."

Robert came back shortly. "The hotel is booked. We can search for another room later today. Let's rest with the door open and then we'll go get some lunch."

As I lay there, my body cramped, "Oh great, my cycle has started."

"I think we should leave this room for a while and go to lunch," Robert replied. "We need fresh air."

From our restaurant table, looking through huge windows. I admired the great view overlooking rooftops and some of the city below. After ordering our meal, Robert and I talked about possible tours. I sat there smiling, so happy to be on vacation. But suddenly, my body heated up so much that I felt like I was going to pass out from the heat, so I started to take my tee shirt off, being half conscious I knew I would be naked. I was being transported down a tunnel of blue light.

I thought, *Oh my God, my life is not passing before me like a movie! I am in a blue light tunnel. This is different than my past two near-death experiences. This may … be it. Is this how I die?*

Cheerfully, the waiter set down the plate of food, and the clinking of the silverware momentarily pulled me back to the restaurant. My body swirling, my face fell towards the plate of food.

The startled waiter grasped anxiously for my shoulders. "Lady you don't need food, you need oxygen. I'll be right back with a tank."

Robert stood up and held me by my shoulders. My chin fell to my chest.

The man came back with a huge steel tank on wheels and stuck a plastic mask on my face. "Breath in the oxygen as long as you like. You may need it for at least ten minutes."

Finally, I came around. Sweating profusely, I ran to the bathroom to check on my blood flow. I was gasping for air while a German girl puffed on her cigarette, filling the room with smoke. I wondered if the universe was setting me up for a difficult trip.

I went back to our table and was able to drink my tea and eat a little bit.

"Robert, I'm feeling a bit better. Since our hotel room is so toxic, maybe we should take a tour. If I feel sick, I could sit somewhere and wait for you. I don't want to ruin your trip."

"Sounds like a plan," he replied.

He found a bus to take us on a three-hour tour around the city. Our first stop was a Catholic church. The tour guide took us down into the basement and outside of the church to show us huge blocks of stone, the church's foundation.

The Inca-looking tour guide informed us: "These huge blocks of stone are the remains of an Incan temple. The Incas cut these stones so precisely they fit together without mortar. During earthquakes, it's now understood that these precise cut stones settle together quite well. Unfortunately, the Incas used mortar in between stones on some of their less important buildings and many of these fell apart during earthquakes."

"Conquerors built their temples over the conquered peoples' temples," she continued. "They also used Inca stone blocks in their other buildings. Now I'll give you some history of the invasion."

Taking a break, I sat on a hard-wooden church bench next to Emma, another girl on our tour. Staring at the wall in front of me, I saw the bloodiest picture I'd ever seen of Christ being tortured on the cross.

I whispered to Emma, "This is pretty torturous, looking at this painting. Were they using this image to threaten the Inca people? Because of my period, high altitude and these cold stonewalls, I'm bleeding profusely. I don't think I'll be able to visit another church in this town."

Emma whispered, "I'm having a terrible time with my period, too. It's painful to look at this. Maybe we should find another place to sit, like on the bus."

"Yea, let's leave this place."

As we were leaving, I reflected, "My favorite image of Christ is one where Christ's heart is emanating Light."

"Thanks for the visual," Emma said. "It makes me feel better."

Emma and I endured the rest of the tour. That evening, Robert and I went to a fine Peruvian restaurant. As he read the menu, he exclaimed, "They have guinea pig on the menu … their native delicacy. I'm going to try it."

Looking startled, I said, "I hope you're joking. Are you trying to make me sick?"

"Where else am I ever going to get to try this?" Robert asked.

I held my breath in shock as the waiter took our order.

"I don't believe you just ordered a rat cooked well done."

"They probably have an interesting way of cooking it," Robert replied, smiling triumphantly.

The waiter came, extending out the plate with the small cooked guinea pig. There it was, full body, upside-down, little feet sticking in the air, reminding me of the dead armadillos along the roadsides in Florida. I wanted to move to another table. Other tourists and local people looked astonished as the waiter set the plate down in front of Robert. Shaking my head, I felt sad for the little rat. Everyone around us watched as Robert picked up his fork and knife to cut into the overcooked creature. His knife was not sharp enough to cut into the meat. He kept trying. I started laughing as did the people around us.

Robert smiled and waved his hand in the air. "Oh waiter, do you have a sharper knife?"

The waiter replied, "Si," while reaching for one off another table.

Everyone watched as Robert took his first bite and chewed it very slowly. He straightened his posture, flashed a smug and approving restaurant critic's smile. He looked around at everyone and said, "It tastes a bit like chicken." Everyone laughed and went back to their dinners.

After we finished our meals, I asked, "So really, how was – your meal? Were you happy with it?"

"It was a bit dry and there wasn't much to eat," Robert replied. "Chicken might have tasted better."

"Well, you entertained a lot of people tonight," I said, giggling almost out of control. "Let's head back to our room."

Robert and I got very little sleep in the stuffy fortress room. With its one tiny barred window located up near the ceiling, the room felt as though it had been an ancient prison cell.

The next morning, we immediately found a more bright and airy modern hotel. However, the water shut off at certain times of day, preventing us from showering. Apparently, the city was in the process of fixing pipes.

Meanwhile, Robert and I read in our tour book about the many ruins encircling the city. We hired an inexpensive cab driver and an English-speaking guide for a long day tour to different ruins.

As we drove towards our first destination, our tour guide, Maria warned us, "There was an article in the paper today about a tourist being pushed over a cliff at one of the sites by a member of the Shining Path. We have three active terrorist groups in Peru right now, the Shining Path being the most active. They want to disrupt the economy by hurting the tourist trade. Irene, your hair is blonde so they'll assume you are from the US. Hug the mountains and don't stand close to cliff edges. If you see a group of boys, go where people are. Everything should be okay, but it's best to be careful."

Despite this, the exploration of ancient ruins and temples filled me with a peaceful, joyous energy. Ancient stories of these places inspired images of hidden treasures and knowledge. I often saw artistic images, symbols similar to those I'd seen or read about from other distant cultures. The ancient peoples were surely connected. I felt a sense of oneness from this realization.

A group of young boys waved their camera at me. Hesitating, I clung near the ruins' wall. Just a few feet on the other side of the narrow path, the cliff side fell at least three hundred feet.

In Spanish, one boy asked, "Will you take our picture?"

Not moving, I reached out my hand for the camera and said, "Yes."

I took a few pictures of them, with all of us laughing.

"We each want our picture with you," one boy said.

I replied, "It'll be ok as long as you don't throw darts at my picture."

Puzzled, they looked at each other. One boy interpreted my words. Then they laughed.

"Oh no, we want to show you as our girlfriend from America."

"Okay," I said. "But we have to stand over here facing the ruins."

They each posed with me and took their pictures. Just as we were finishing, I saw Robert running towards us with concern.

I yelled, wanting to slow him down, "Everything is alright, we're only taking pictures."

The boys dispersed as Robert arrived.

Many of the ruins around Cusco had been damaged, their artwork defaced or robbed by the Spanish, tourists, and time. We didn't spend that much time at the individual ruins, but it was fun seeing them as we drove through the region.

Late in the day, we arrived at our hotel. While eating at a nearby restaurant, we shared our day's musings, loving our private tour. We decided to spend our last day shopping and walking about town.

Finally, we were on our train ride to Machu Picchu.

Leaving his seat, Robert said, "I'm going to see if we can get better views of the jungle somewhere else on the train."

He returned looking excited.

"I found two empty seats in the front of the train. The front car has a large wide curving window. The views are awesome."

We gathered our luggage and moved to those seats. After a few minutes the train stopped. No one got on, no one got off. We noticed men checking the train tracks.

Then a train conductor came by, looking upset. "You can't sit in this car. This car is for this special group of people."

We went back to our seats. A few minutes later, the train stopped again. We saw the *special* people stepping out of the first car and walking into the jungle. Again, men were checking the tracks. Robert wandered off.

As soon as the train started, Robert came back to our seats.

"Irene, let's go back to the front car. No one's there now. It's empty." Again, we gathered our luggage.

Incredible views of the jungle rushed by us. "Wow, Robert! This is like a thrilling E ticket ride at Disneyland, except the jungle is real."

He exclaimed, "Yee-haw!"

The train stopped again. Men were checking the tracks. The conductor walked by us, but just smiled this time.

"If they have terrorist groups," I said, "maybe, they're checking the train tracks for bombs. We should ask the conductor. The front of the train is where the first-class people would sit, and that would be the part to blow up first."

"Irene, you're so suspicious," Robert said.

"Hey, I'm careful and I think like a detective."

As the conductor walked by, Robert asked, "Sir, why is the train stopping so often, and why are the men checking around the tracks?"

"We inspect the tracks every so often. It's routine."

Robert looked at me. "Feel better?"

"Not really, but I might as well enjoy the moment." I said a silent prayer asking God to please protect us and the other people on the train. I invoked the divine light, blessing myself, my parents, my teachers, my extended family, all the peoples of the Earth, the jungle with all its fauna and animals, all the beings and elements of the Earth, blessing the universe and the Supreme Universal Being which is my innermost indwelling spirit. Filled with bliss, I felt safe once more.

Once we arrived, we took the tram with our luggage up to the hotel closest to the Machu Picchu site. We checked into the hotel quickly, so we could explore the ruins as much as possible before nightfall.

We signed up for the next tour. As we gathered around the tour guide, she pointed at the beautiful surrounding mountain peaks.

"As you can see, this site is nestled on this mountain ridge at 7,970 feet, overlooking the Urubamba Valley. That beautiful mountain peak over there is her sister mountain, Huayna Picchu. If you're here tomorrow, you'll be able to hike up her trail to the top and have another view of Machu Picchu."

All the tourists looked in awe.

Fig. 75 Machu Picchu, Peru

Fig. 76 Irene is hiking on Huayna Picchu.

She continued, "Machu Picchu is a pre-Columbian site. The Incas built this site around 1450. Some people say that the inhabitants all died after catching small pox from the Spanish. Most of the site is intact since the Spanish conquistadors never found it. Some say it was a religious site. Its temples were built with huge, precisely cut stones. There's still evidence of an irrigation system from the springs to bring water to the homes. In 1911, Hiram Bingham, an explorer and historian from the United States, told stories about Machu Picchu's beauty, bringing its attention to the world. He, along with others, looted the place over the years. Some amends have been made to bring precious objects back to Peru. Please walk around carefully as you explore the ruins."

It was a magnificent sight. We walked around and then found a rock to sit upon and meditate in the ancient energy.

The next morning, after a hearty breakfast of eggs and toast, Robert and I trekked over to Huayna Picchu. We soon realized the trail wasn't marked well.

As hikers came down the trail, I asked, "Is this the way up?"

Parts of the path were steep and washed out from rains. At one point, I saw an ancient stone archway. As I ran towards it, a voice in my head told me to slow down. Just as I entered the archway, I saw a drop-off, thousands of feet down. It was a gorgeous view, but frightening.

"My God, Robert, they should've put a sign here warning of the drop off."

"Obviously, it's not like American parks. We're on our own. So be careful."

As we climbed higher and higher, I grew tired.

"I sure hope someone is at the top of this mountain selling cokes or something sweet. I need an energy boost," I said. Sweat dripped down my face and my clothes clung to my body. The heat and humidity were becoming overwhelming.

"Dream on girl. Do you think anyone would be willing to carry a heavy thing of cokes up this mountain?"

"At last, we made it to the top," I sung out. Robert and I both started laughing. Before our eyes stood a hearty built, Inca man selling sodas and water out of a huge ice chest.

As I happily drank down my coke, Robert said, "Well Irene, I guess dreams do come true." Pointing, he said, "Go sit out on that rock overlooking the valley below, so I can get your picture."

As I climbed towards the rock, I could see 7,000 feet down, clear to the river. Feeling a bit woozy, I sat down as soon as I reached the edge. I realized that since I had known Robert, I had had my picture taken on a number of dangerous precipices.

Robert yelled, "Irene, go more over on the other edge of the rock."

I yelled, "You're crazy. I'm sitting tight. You can come out here and I'll take a picture of you hanging over. Just give me your wallet first."

Watching our antics, another couple burst out laughing. I took several pictures of Robert. As he climbed back to the level area, I reminded him that we needed to plant our prayer flags. We had written prayers and bound them to sticks with colored yarns the way some native tribes do. Robert pulled them out of his backpack. As we looked around for a place to plant them into the ground, the Inca vendor asked in Spanish to look at them. I handed him one, putting my hands together in prayer position, to let him know what they were.

Shaking his head, he said, "Si."

He pointed to a spot where they could be safely stuck into the ground. Then he pointed to his belt and said, "Ten Commandments."

"Look Robert, I said, "his belt has silver disks with each of the Ten Commandments. We plant Indian prayer sticks and the Inca Indian wears a belt symbolizing the Ten Commandments. How cool is that?"

The three of us gave each other the prayer hand sign before Robert and I headed back down the mountain.

Next stop was Lima. It was Thanksgiving Day in America. Robert and I were eating breakfast in a large hotel in Lima when all the lights went out.

The waiter came over to our table. "It'll be a few minutes before our auxiliary electricity comes on. The Shining Path warned us that they were going to knock out Lima's main electric facility."

Worried, I looked over at Robert. "I sure hope that we can get a bus today to go to the archeological site of the Nazca Lines. Can you imagine how fun it will be to see the large animal drawings from up in the air?"

"Let's get out of here, for sure," he replied, concerned.

We walked over to the concierge.

I asked, "How can we get to the Nazca Lines?"

She said, "Tour buses are too dangerous right now. The banditos have been stopping tour busses and robbing everyone. No planes are available. I might be able to get you a taxi driver who could drive you around for two days. But with the electricity out, most of the gas pumps in the city aren't working. I'll make some phone calls. Come back in half an hour."

Determined to leave Lima, Robert and I went back to the room and quickly packed our bags. We went back to the concierge.

AWAKENING LOVE'S VIBRATIONS

"You're lucky. I found a taxi driver. Miguel speaks English, so he'll also be a good tour guide. His wife is a schoolteacher. For a reasonable amount of money, he'll be able to drive you to the Nazca Lines. You can stay over one night at a small hotel. The next morning you can fly over the lines in a helicopter or a small plane. Then he'll drive you back to Lima. He can be here in a half hour. So, do you want to go?"

I said, "Yes, we want to go. Thank you so much."

Robert and I quickly checked out of the hotel and headed back to the concierge's desk.

Finally, after waiting over an hour with Miguel at a gas station that had a hand pump, we were on our journey. We passed many sand dunes. The terrain was very desert-like. At times, we saw the ocean.

Miguel said, "If a bandito or a police officer stops the car, I'll make up a story to protect us. I may have to give them a few dollars to let us pass. Hopefully, we'll be able to drive straight through with no one bothering us."

As he talked, I stuck most of my dollars, traveler's checks, and my diamond ring in my sock. I left a few bills and some traveler's checks in my money belt. As Robert watched me, I smirked and raised my eyebrows. "Better to be safe."

Arriving safely at our hotel, we made plans for the next morning. I was so excited about flying over the Nazca Lines that I barely slept.

The next morning after breakfast, Miguel drove us to a tiny airfield. Robert and I sat in the back seat of the small airplane. The pilot and a tour guide sat in the front seat.

The pilot turned his head and looked at me. "Are you okay with flying?"

I replied, "Let's get this plane in the air!"

As the plane flew, the tour guide pointed out images of different figures, geometric shapes, animals and birds made of thick lines, far below us. *These people must have had flying machines,* I thought, *or else they were beckoning to someone in outer space.*

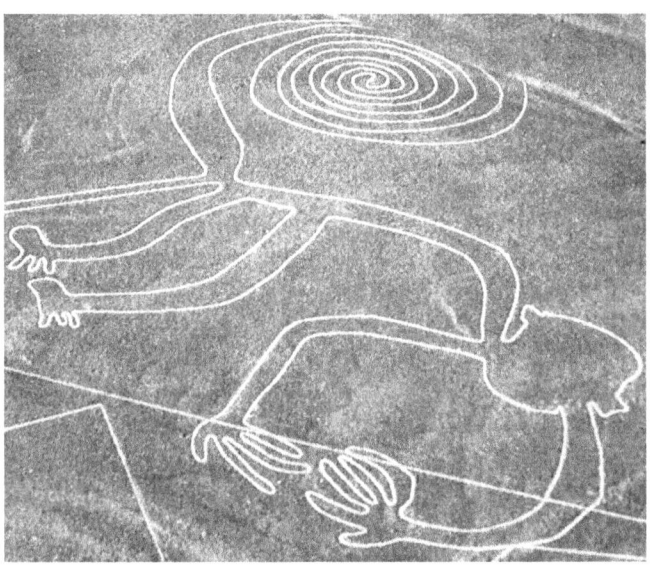 

Fig. 77 - Left - Nazca Lines, Peru – monkey image, view from the airplane.
Fig. 78 - Right - Astronaut image as seen from an airplane.

The tour guide interrupted my thoughts, saying, "The Nazca Lines are known as the most outstanding group of ancient geoglyphs in the world. They are etched into our sand. There's a layer of small dark reddish pebbles over a lighter colored soil. There are many theories about their creation and size. One is that the Nazca people wanted the Gods in the sky to see them. Other people say it was a type of spiritual ritual for the people to walk along the lines. Some people felt they would have needed a flying machine to create them. However, the Nazca people were known as excellent weavers of cloth. It was recently proven that by using a weaver's design, they could mathematically make it larger and then use string and posts to plot out the design on a grand scale. These people followed the ropes, exposing the soil below, creating large scale art images."

I starred at the figures below, marveling at the mysteries. As soon as the plane landed, we had lunch, and then headed back to Lima.

Seemingly out of nowhere, a uniformed man with a large rifle flagged down our car. Our taxi driver talked with him for a few minutes, handed him a few dollars, and we were on our way.

Our taxi driver said, "I told him you were ambassadors and needed to get to Lima right away. I told him he shouldn't delay your trip."

I didn't think it was good to make us important, but I trusted Miguel's judgment. After all, we were safe so far. During the ride home, Miguel told us that he and his wife had given up one of their daughters to a wealthy American couple. The couple promised she would get an education, that they would treat her well. They sent his family money and they let Miguel and his wife visit her every few years.

With tears in his eyes, he said, "I really miss my daughter, but I know that this is best for everyone. Life can be so hard here."

As he spoke, I cried for his loss. I knew only too well the difficulties of growing up in poverty. "I'll say prayers for your family to be reunited."

Finally, we arrived in Lima. Miguel made sure that we were able to get a room in a nice hotel. Having become friends in those few short days, we found it difficult to say goodbye.

The next day we caught a bus to take us to Puno, Peru, a small city on the edge of Lake Titicaca. Lake Titicaca is 12,500 ft. above sea level, making it the highest commercially navigable lake in South America. From the sky, the shape of the lake looks like a puma chasing a rabbit. We visited the floating reed islands where many local indigenous people reside and sell their crafts. Many of the children had large open sores showing on their legs and arms. I struggled to hold back my tears. I bought some of their crafts even though I was concerned about touching the objects. The smells from the rotting reeds made my stomach feel nauseated.

In the morning, we headed on a bus to La Paz, Bolivia. Barren rock strewn mountains and dry dessert land loomed alongside us. Just as we were about twenty miles from the border, our bus stopped and the driver got out to inspect the situation.

"We have a problem," the driver announced. "The Bolivian people are rebelling against their government. They've knocked large boulders and rocks off the nearby mountains, blocking the road for over a mile. I've called the tourist office and I'm waiting for a reply on what to do next."

Meanwhile, I had to pee, badly. There were no trees. I saw only one large rock.

Finally, I spoke up and said, "I have to go pee. What do I do?"

He looked dumbfounded. "We're going to be here for a while."

Another woman said, "I have to go, too. I think we should go behind that rock."

As I scanned the mountainside, I said, "But there are men standing around on the hillsides."

Another woman chimed in, "We'll form a circle facing outward until we've all finished."

That resolved that issue. It was so hot, maybe a hundred degrees or more, and we were dehydrated. Finally, some enterprising young man showed up with a cooler of bottled water.

After an hour went by, the bus driver said, "The tourist office is sending another bus. It'll wait on the other side of this boulder-laden road. So, in a half hour, we'll take your luggage off the bus and you need to walk it to the other side. For a dollar, some of the local people will carry it for you. They are strong people."

I paid a Bolivian man a dollar to carry my suitcase. These short stocky men put the suitcases on their backs to carry them. I showed him that my suitcase had wheels and he needed only to lift it now and then. He wheeled it for a little bit, until his macho friends started laughing and making fun of him, so he resumed carrying it on his back. Soon however, he rolled it, laughing at his friends.

Robert and I were happy to make it to the other side to the new bus. We arrived late at night in the city of La Paz. The next day we took a private tour to Tiwanaku, a pre-Columbian, pre-Incan site dating back to 600 BC. Tiwanaku was a sacred ceremonial and political site. Some people believe Tiwanaku's culture to be even more advanced than the Incans'. Our tour guide then took us to some lesser-known sites in the area. She told us that the local people dug up artifacts and sold them. However, they were masters of making replicas look old. So, we were warned to only buy what we liked and to not overpay for any clay pottery.

As I walked around the dusty ruins, I felt joy bubble up inside of me as my imagination took flight. *Perhaps, I might have missed a calling to be an archeologist,* I wondered. A few venders wandered over to me unwrapping little clay sculptures from their worn-out newspaper coverings. Trying to hide my delight at seeing the quality and beauty of the sculptures, I bargained a bit and bought seven pieces. I thought that if a present-day artist replicated these so finely, they deserved to earn a good living.

CHAPTER TWENTY-FOUR

The Cat's Dream Comes True

FINALLY, AFTER THAT ADVENTUROUS JOURNEY, I had settled back into my routine. One night, I noticed that my little gray Persian cat, Purrsha, looked sluggish. I decided I would take her to the veterinarian that evening, after work.

As I was leaving for work, I walked into Roberts office. "Robert, please don't let Purrsha go outside today. She looks sick."

While staring at his computer screen, Robert said, "Okay."

When I got home from work, I searched the house for Purrsha.

I called out, "Where's Purrsha?"

"She's outside somewhere," replied Robert.

Upset, I looked outside in her usual playing places. My other cat, Fang was chasing birds on the roof of our single level house. Purrsha was usually with him. Searching the neighborhood, I posted on poles and handed out posters with Purrsha's picture and my information. Finally, after two days, a neighbor called and said, "I think I may have your cat. I was just watering my plants and saw a small gray cat in my bush. Do you want to come for her? She is all wet and looks sick. I'm located two houses down from your house."

"I'll be right there!" I grabbed a soft carrying case with a clean towel and ran to the woman's house. Purrsha was wet and barely breathing. Quickly, I drove her to an animal hospital, telling her softly how much I loved her. They needed to keep her overnight. It was difficult for me to leave her.

The next morning, I drove immediately to the animal clinic. The girl at the desk said, "I'm sorry we did everything we could, but she died in the night. Please follow me. Wait here. The doctor will be right with you."

The doctor came into the room. Reaching out his hand, he said, "I'm sorry for your loss. We did various tests and discovered that she had licked up anti-freeze that had leaked out of someone's car. It turned her urine to crystals, killing her. There was nothing more we could do."

I stood there frozen in shock with tears rolling down my face. Then I remembered that Robert's truck had been parked outside and was leaking something. I thought, *Oh, my God, I'd better protect Fang. I hope it's not too late for him.*

Barely audible words filtered through to me. The veterinarian said, "Anti-freeze … tastes sweet to animals … many die from drinking it. It's better to make cats…indoor pets. Let me know soon, what you would like to do with Purrsha's body. Please pay your bill at the front desk."

The girl handed me a bill tallying $500.00 dollars. Shocked even more, raising my eyebrows, shaking with grief and anger, feeling ripped off, I said, "Holy shit! How can you charge me so much? Why didn't you tell me in advance how expensive your prices are?"

"You'd have left your cat anyway."

"Yes, I'd have left my cat. But, you left me clueless, that the bill could be this high for one night.

She said, "Cash or charge it on a credit card?"

"Here's my card. I'll come back for her ashes. No special box."

I hurried home, ran into the garage and found some driveway cleaner and scrubbed the antifreeze and hosed it down. That night I told Robert he needed to put cardboard under his truck and put it in his truck when he drove around until he could get it fixed on his next free day. I didn't want any more animals hurt.

For over two weeks, I cried and cried. I didn't know how to handle my grief. I feared waiting on customers at the jewelry store, thinking I was going to break out in tears during the sales presentation. I finally realized that, in the process of grieving, I wasn't available for the people around me. I wasn't able to be compassionate to others. Everyone had always told me that grieving is a process and takes time. I started to think grieving was a bit selfish, especially if I wasn't available to help others. However, I didn't know how to stop my inner pain.

That night before I went to sleep, I prayed, "Please God, let me know that my cat's spirit is all right and help me to be present for myself and others."

While in a deep sleep, a lucid dream came to me. I was walking along a path in a beautiful tropical jungle, a full moon illuminating the path and a rich cluster of exotic flowers. The sky was a deep indigo. Stars twinkled through the treetops. Purrsha's large golden eyes sparkled as she sat serenely upon a tree branch. As I gazed lovingly at Purrsha, she transformed into a multicolored owl-like bird with large golden eyes. She flew into the sky. Seeing her spirit set free, I woke up with a deep feeling of peace.

At breakfast, I asked, "Robert do you think that when cats chase birds, the cats wish they could fly? Humans have always wanted to fly."

"I guess animals might get jealous that birds can fly. They seem to have some degree of consciousness. You look cheerful this morning."

I told Robert about my dream. Then we each went off to work. I had a blissful happy day, thanking God for the dream.

That evening when I arrived home, another magical event occurred. My cat, Fang, whose favorite pastime was chasing birds on our roof, was acting strange. He was jumping in and out of the cat door leading from the house to the garage. He would stop and stare at me, as if wanting me to follow him. When I opened the door, I saw an opened newspaper on the floor. Fang kept tapping it with his paw. I lifted up the newspaper and screamed, mainly from surprise. There on the floor was a colorful peach-faced lovebird. The bird looked stunned, but Fang hadn't killed it. Usually Fang left dissected parts of his prey around. I put the bird in a small box on a clean cloth with a little bowl of water.

Then I called Robert's mom, who loved birds, and asked her how I should take care of it. She brought over a cage and some food.

I was stunned. On that same day that I'd woken up from a dream in which Purrsha turned into a multicolored bird, Fang had caught a colorful bird and didn't hurt it. *Can a cat see in color? Did he realize that this bird was special? Was Fang psychic and had he tapped into my dream?* The universe was so amazing, blending dreamtime and daytime.

After a few days, I noticed Fang glaring a lot at our newly named bird, Peachy. Fang seemed to be having misgivings and just might figure out how to kill our new little friend. I felt that Peachy was the universe's gift of confirmation that Purrsha's spirit was all right. It was a difficult decision, but I gave Peachy to Robert's mom. She loved birds and knew how to care for them. She taught Peachy to talk.

I realized from this experience that Divine Grace is always present. I felt that Divine Grace was the highest, lightest of energy vibrations, love permeating all space; we just needed to whole-heartedly invite her into our being.

A few years later, as an attempt to depict my dream, I painted *The Cat's Dream Comes True*. Starting on a piece of raw unstretched canvas approximately 50" high by 30" wide, I painted a huge owl with outstretched wings perched on a tree branch, with a cat with open wings, sitting right in front of the owl. Their outstretched wings symbolized "openness" (as when I open my arms to welcome another person) and taking flight to the Heavens.

The owl was painted red and gold. The gold color symbolized royalty and other worldliness, while the red color depicted passion and Mother Earth. I gave the owl golden eyes like the bird in my dream. Purrsha also had beautiful golden eyes. I used my new Siamese cat, Coco as my model for the cat's image. His face had an ancient and dignified look.

In the cat's chest was an oval egg-shaped hole, showing another world within him. Within the hole, I painted the ouroboros (a snake with its tail in its mouth) symbolizing eternity as well as the marriage of light and dark.

I painted the cat's body a blue gray with a touch of violet, red, and gold. Where the cat's wings met the owl's wings I added red and gold, making them airy to blend with the owl's wings. The basic blue of the cat represented the heavens.

The cat's tail I painted as a spiral showing sacred energy. At the end of the tree branch, I painted the six-sided star as the union of heaven and earth, which for me was the meaning of the whole painting. The cat and snake are of the earth as the owl is of the sky. Red is the earth and blue is the sky.

Part way through the painting, I added sand to polymer medium using it to blend the sand strokes with the feathers and to add texture to the sky. Since sand is made of tiny quartz crystals, I added them for their energetic alchemy effect. Final layers were painted with oil paint. I left the painting unstretched for a long time, liking the primitiveness of it. After some time, I decided to glue it on top of a larger, stretched canvas and paint a blending border. After I finished the painting and saw it in the natural daylight, I was amazed at its soft shimmering quality. There appeared to be a magical alchemy between the quartz crystals and the transparent layers of oil paint.

AWAKENING LOVE'S VIBRATIONS

Fig. 79 Vincent, *The Cat's Dream Comes True*, started a few years after the dream in 1989, 60"H x 47 ½"W, Repainted 2007, oil over acrylic and sand on canvas.

CHAPTER TWENTY-FIVE

Being Healed by Light and Yoga

FLASHING BACK TO ONE VERY HOT humid summer in Rochester, New York when I was 18 years old, and working in a small plastic print factory around toxic chemicals, I remembered a small group of us wiping ink off misprinted plastic bottles with acetone and benzene. The temperature inside the small building ranged from 90 degrees to 115 degrees. The evaporating fumes pierced our nostrils. We were given plastic gloves that dissolved quickly, exposing our hands. When the company ran out of plastic gloves, they wanted us to continue using the benzene-filled rags with our bare hands, toxifying our skin.

Finally, I pulled the boss aside and said, "Look, my hands and nostrils are burning. If you don't have gloves and proper ventilation, you need to move me to another task. There must be a law against this kind of treatment."

She said, "I know conditions aren't perfect. But this company is a small subsidiary of a larger corporation. It doesn't have a union and it doesn't have to follow the same rules as the larger corporation. This is how large corporations save money."

Standing there with tears in my eyes, I knew I was going back to college, that I could and would quit this job. The other people were supporting their families. They were scared to speak up.

"There must be something you can do to help us," I said,

"I'll set up fans and try to blow the evaporating fumes away from your faces," she said. "I'll not force you to work without gloves. And I'll try not to give you this task on days this hot. We ran out of clean bottles and we need to get this order finished today."

A few weeks later, I quit the job.

Afterwards, I suffered from poor digestion, bloating, and difficulty breathing. I experienced bouts of extreme pain. I'd awaken in the middle of the night and throw up. I kept eliminating foods from my diet.

Then, three years after I'd left that horrible job, I was visiting my family in Rochester. I was walking through Sibley's department store when I heard someone call my name. It was Juan. He was a tall thin handsome man in his thirty's. He was always smiling, carrying an inner happiness.

Juan said, "Hey, Irene, do you remember me from the plastic print factory?"

"Sure Juan. How are you?"

"You know, that shortly after you left, Mary, who had only worked there for three years came down with bladder cancer and died a few months later. It scared me and I quit," he said.

"I really liked Mary. That's a bit shocking. I'm glad you quit. I haven't felt well since I worked at that place. I recently read about the possible effects of over breathing acetone and benzene fumes, finding they could possible cause bladder or liver cancer."

"Well, I found a better paying job that I like," he said.

"That's great Juan. Good to see you. If you bump into any of our other old co-workers let them know that they might be hurting their health working there."

"I will. Until we meet again," he said, still smiling, continuing with his shopping.

I was concerned, but just hoped that whatever ailed me would go away. Over the years, the pain returned once every few months, but then increased to once a week, then every night. Not good about going to doctors, I decided to go to an Iridologist, who could diagnose disease from examining a picture of my eyes. He said that I had a gall bladder problem and perhaps a liver problem. I drank a concoction of olive oil and lemon juice that a friend recommended for gallstones, which I'd also read about in one of my books on healing. I passed a kidney stone and might have passed gallstones. I felt better. However, I was still sick and now in my late twenties.

When I was about 36, Ron, my business partner told me he heard about a Persian healer named Mehri who healed people with light and energy. He was going to take a few sessions with her to see if he felt better. She was coming to our area for two months. Otherwise, we'd have to drive sixty miles to Los Angeles to get a healing.

Shortly thereafter, I met Mehri. She suggested I sign up for six healing sessions. She told me that in Persia, she had been a surgeon, until she noticed that she actually healed people faster with heat from her hands. When she came to the US, she only healed people with this heat energy. I had some doubts, but kept an open mind.

I lay on a cot as she slowly moved her hands above me. I could feel her energy. It was very delicate and soothing, deeply relaxing. After the six sessions, I was back to eating everything that I had previously enjoyed in my life.

Yoga was also paramount in healing me. When I was twenty, I was a passenger in a car struck from behind. My neck was injured. Over the years, I went to different chiropractors for any kind of relief. Then, as I earned more income, I was able to afford massages that helped relax me, and that healed my neck. As I practiced Yoga postures, I became more relaxed and flexible. My bodily awareness grew more acute. In the past, if I became tense, my neck would get stuck in a position, and would take days to limber up. As a result of my yoga practice, I could feel when my neck was about to twist a muscle, so I would gently stop the movement, breathe, and relax. I no longer had to suffer for weeks with a stiff neck.

Likewise, when I did my freeform stretching dance in the morning, I'd stretch through where my body ached, and where it had stiffened in the night. In the past, if I woke up with a stiff hip in the morning, it would only worsen during the daytime. Now I released the stiffness, and felt great all day long. After a while, it was rare that I felt any bodily pains.

CHAPTER TWENTY-SIX

Feeling Abundant and The Astrologer

I**N THE GRAND PLAY OF LIFE,** our poverty can change to abundance and our abundance can change to poverty, often times without notice. From my new spiritual teachers, I had learned that the only unchanging thing in our lives is our innermost indwelling spirit. At times, I lived under the illusion that my inner spark was barely lit. Growing up in poverty, under Rochester's gloomy skies tended to depress and sadden me. Paradoxically, I held faith that life's circumstances would improve.

As I grew into my twenties, I felt an ache in my heart for myself and for the world. I sometimes felt as though I had a black hole in my heart, a sentiment echoed in the book, *The Fire from Within* by Carlos Castaneda. As I read his words, I realized that from experiencing all these self-awareness classes, saying prayers, practicing energy moving exercises, and, most of all, meeting these love-emanating spiritual teachers that my heart had filled with love and light – the greatest abundance I'd ever felt. In feeling all this joy, I wanted the same for everyone. I hoped that by meditating, by praying, and by keeping my life in balance, I too could build up a spiritual vibration that emanated love to others.

I thought, *What greater gift could I give to the world? Will I be able to do this as an ordinary person, outside of a monastic system? Only time will tell.*

In 1988, along with this new spiritual abundance, our business grew, increasing my income. Our jewelry boutique had been less than 370 square feet. With the store behind us going out of business, however, we were able to knock down walls, and increase the square footage to 1800.

I told Ron I wanted to design the new addition to our store. Ron asked me to draw it all out quickly and prove to him that it was indeed a good design that would meet our needs. On draft paper, I redesigned the layout of the store, the showcases, the locations for four safes, and all the displays for the jewelry. Everything was designed to show off the maximum amount of jewelry. Ron hired our mentor friend Susan Christopher to come by the store, look at my drawings, and help us decide if they worked. Susan gave her approval.

We had gone from three employees to six full-time and three part-time employees, so new store policy books were a must. Ron and I both felt like we needed to be psychologists to train and manage our employees, so he hired Susan to help us write up our company's mission statement and our store's policy books. Once this was done, we were able to grow our business faster than we ever thought possible. We opened ourselves to different sales and management courses in order to improve our business.

We made one employee a manager, and eventually added an assistant manager. Most of the time either Ron or I were present in the store. A few times a year we would have Susan give a lecture to our employees on salesmanship and teamwork.

Making the business more successful was a vital part of me gaining more freedom to paint and practice my spirituality. And when we got a break to advertise on television, Ron turned out to be a genius at directing and getting the right people to make our commercials. All this helped take our business to the next level.

Buying a larger house, one with a guest room for spiritual teachers, now seemed like an option. Moving in the next year or two had been my plan, but then, one sunny day the universe prepared me for faster movement.

While I was visiting Yogananda's Gardens in Encinitas, California, the overall serenity filled my heart with peace. Colorful flowers covered the grounds. Taking time to meditate, I sat for a while on a bench overlooking the Pacific Ocean, every so often gazing at the vibrant green water filled with a million pin points of twinkling light. On my way through the gardens, I also, sat and prayed near a Koi pond, watching the golden and orange fish swim gracefully through the water, their lips breaking the surface, splashing ever so quietly. A beautiful green blue iridescent dragonfly flittered by me.

After the Gardens, I decided to explore some shops that lined the main street of town. One shopkeeper offered a fifteen-minute astrology reading for twenty dollars. I was going through some changes, and I thought I could possibly get some guidance.

As John, the astrologer looked at my birth chart, he said, "Irene, it looks as though you'll be moving in the next three to six months."

I replied, "I've too much work right now. Maybe, in a year or two."

"Irene, if you don't move, the universe will cause you to move."

I grew agitated. "How's that possible?"

"Well, what caused you to leave your last location?"

"I was living in a warehouse and the neighbors got noisy and were belligerent."

"What are the conditions for you now?"

Reflecting a moment, I replied, "Oh my God, the neighbor has just started playing country and western music at full volume at 2 o'clock in the morning. The music blasts horrible bass sounds right through my garage door. Somehow it amplifies the sound right into my bedroom. One night it was so painful that I got out of bed and walked over to her house in my nightgown. When I pounded on her front door, it swung open."

"I stood there yelling, 'Hello, hello! Is anybody home? Can you turn down the music?' No one could hear me. I kept on yelling. The loud music caused a painful vibration inside my body, making my heartbeat go out of sync. I grew angry, my muscles tensing as I stood there. I thought, *Do I go back home and bare it? Do I call the police? Do I walk into her house a little more to see if she can hear me? Oh shit, I'm going to risk it.*

"I walked through the entry to her kitchen, where I yelled, 'Turn down the music! Turn down the music! Turn down the music!'

"After the third yell, I heard a man ask her, 'Did you hear someone?'

"'No, but go and check the door.'

"The man came into the kitchen and was shocked to see me. He asked, 'What are you doing in here?'

"'I've been yelling over and over for you to turn down the music, but you couldn't hear me because it's so damn loud. I live directly across the street and this is the second night this week you've woken me up. I have to work in the morning.'

"He turned his head, 'It's your neighbor, sweetheart. Turn the music down.'

"She barely lowered it and ran into the kitchen. With a slurred voice, she asked, 'What are you doing in my house? I could have shot you.'

"Trying to contain my building rage, I said, 'Your door was ajar. When I pounded on it, it flew open. Your music is amplifying through my garage door. This is the second time this week you've woken me up. Would you rather I call the police? I didn't want to come over here in the middle of the night.'

"Staggering, but trying to hold herself up, she said, 'Oh, we're just partying. I didn't realize my music was so loud.'

"I looked her straight in the eyes and said, 'Well, you're going to have to turn the volume down a lot lower than it is, right now.'

"As I headed out the front door, I heard her say, 'Sorry, I didn't realize it was loud.'"

I ran across the street to my house, shivering. *Wow*, I thought, *that was pretty stupid She was drunk and probably did have a gun.*

I looked at the astrologer, "Sorry I was so long winded. I tried to bury that recent event. Other irritating things are happening, too. You may be right about me moving."

Our time was up.

As I was leaving, I said, "I sure hope the universe gives me more time at my house."

He smiled and shook his head.

Within a week, as I was driving to the jewelry store for our weekly meeting, I saw a sign on the freeway in huge letters: "New Homes in Laguna Niguel … Come See the Models". I thought, *If I get out of work early enough, I'll stop by and check out the homes. It'll prepare me with information for when I'm ready.*

Later that day, I visited the models. I saw a beautiful home with four bedrooms and a huge, high-ceiling bonus room. This bonus room would make a great artist studio. I wouldn't have to paint in the garage anymore, suffering the elements. I'd also be closer to work, and to the fresh ocean air.

I asked the manager, "How much income do I need to buy this home? How much is the down payment?"

While writing down facts and numbers on a paper, he said, "Here you go. According to what you've told me, you have to find out what your home is worth and you may be able to buy this model. However, there's high demand and we're having a lottery for the homes and their locations. You need to hold your place in the lottery with a three-thousand-dollar check. As long as you call us once a week, you'll hold your number. The homes will be ready to move into in three to four months."

AWAKENING LOVE'S VIBRATIONS

I had to keep myself from dancing. I went back and called realtors and found out that the housing market was going up. It was an easy time to sell my home. My accountant told me it was a great financial move. My home sold within three weeks and the buyers let me rent until my new home was built. Within four months' time, in September 1988, the universe moved Robert and I into our new home in Laguna Niguel. I loved it and was willing to work hard for this new environment. Never in my wildest dreams, did I ever think I'd own such a fine home.

Other than paintings on the walls and a large semicircular couch, the living room and dining room were unfurnished which allowed Robert the space to teach Iyengar style Hatha yoga one night a week. Women from work and other acquaintances showed up. And this room was great for yogis to give lectures.

Swami Shantanand and his girlfriend Sushil rented a room in the new house for three months. Every week, on Wednesday nights, people came to hear Swami's spiritual lectures. Then Swami and Sushil moved to their New York home. I started feeling a slight void, even before they left.

One day I stopped in my tracks in my downstairs hallway. I suddenly remembered my dream of wanting to create a type of healing center where intellectuals could come give lectures. It always seemed as if I could never quite get enough money together to make it happen. The intellectuals I craved to know and experience were turning into spiritual teachers. It was a "eureka" experience. My soul was crying out for spiritual knowledge and wisdom. I thought how lucky I was to now have a home large enough to invite spiritual teachers to stay, experience them one on one, and sponsor them to give spiritual lectures.

Carlos, one of Swami Vishnudevanand's disciples called me and asked if Swami could come and stay at my house for three weeks in May 1989 and then for three weeks in July 1989. During these summer visits, he would also stay with an Indian family outside of New York City. Swami would give lectures. I invited all the people and cooked huge pots of vegetarian curry for the guests.

After agreeing with Carlos, we made plans for Swami's trip. Every three weeks I received a beautiful inspiring spiritual letter from Swami that read, "Dear Effulgent Radiant Spiritual Soul …". His words were poetic, spiritual poetic love letters to my soul. In coming home from work, and seeing one of his letters waiting for me, I'd immediately find a comfortable spot to sit and savor every word, a wave of bliss washing over me, I couldn't wait for his arrival.

CHAPTER TWENTY-SEVEN

What's Up with Peace?

AFTER ARRIVING HOME ONE EVENING from a hellish day at work, I jumped into a soothing hot shower. Water sprayed gently over my skin, washing away the stickiness of the day's misunderstandings. Once clean, I played some flowing new age electronic music and stretched through my aches and pains, forming a beautiful dance. Then I laid flat upon the floor, talking myself through a ten-minute guided meditation, relaxing my body, visualizing myself walking in a garden, smelling a peach scent from my favorite orange-pink roses.

After that, I sat on my meditation seat which was covered by an indigo blue silk cloth with golden threads. In front of it, sacred objects were arranged on a small wooden bed tray. This special space lay in the alcove of my bedroom. Adorning the towering walls, were my 12ft. triangular painting: *Seeking Oneness* and Tibetan tankas (scrolled Buddhist paintings), creating a Tantric Temple. Seated in meditation, I visualized myself in nature with my back leaning against a huge ancient oak tree. Feeling secure, I drifted off into silence.

Finally, my mind stopped. Thoughts disappeared. Peace at last. Hearing only the sound of my breath, in my mind's eye, my body filled with light.

Suddenly, I felt a rush of energy hit me from across the room, pulling me out of my inward space. I opened my eyes, seeing Robert hurrying through the wide two-door entry into the bedroom.

"Hi Sweetheart," I said. "I was just relaxing after a hard day. I need a few more minutes before we discuss dinner."

He looked at me with angry eyes. Then he said briskly, "I love you."

I questioned, *Am I hallucinating? How can he be saying I love you when he looks so mean?*

Then he blurted, "When I save up enough money, I'm buying my own home."

Taking a deep breath to relieve pangs of confusion and anxiety, I said, "Well, I hope you invite me to live in your home." *I felt sick to my stomach. He hardly contributed. Is he using me as a stepping-stone? Why couldn't he say, I'll rent it out and contribute to our life together or something.*

He said, "We've been living together for almost six years now. In another year and a half, I'll own half of everything you own. You know there is a thing called common law marriage."

"Robert, are you hearing yourself speak? I've worked extremely hard and long hours for what I have, long before and after I've met you. I've been generous to you."

"Well a man needs to have more money than his woman."

"Oh, so will you love me more, if I give you half of my estate?"

"Probably," he said, in a hesitant, unconvincing tone.

Feeling hurt, I said, "By the way Robert, I'm not going to argue with you anymore."

Looking dumbfounded, he asked, "What do you mean? How can we not fight?"

"I've decided to value 'peace' more than my opinions. I refuse to be stressed out from arguing. You can be right if that's important to you. It's one thing to have a creative discussion and search for some form of truth or possibilities about something, but if I see you take a hard stand on a topic, you win."

"There you go switching levels on me, I don't know what you're talking about." He turned and headed out of the room.

Raising my voice a notch, I added, "And I'm not going to go visit your mom anymore. You always manage to get us into a political argument that you set up. She likes to fight. You go visit her by yourself."

"Okay, I won't ask you to visit her anymore," he said reticently.

Thoughts of the day rushed back into my mind. I thought about the horrible things and hurt feelings that had happened during the day at work. My skin felt like the washed off gooey substance had jumped back on it. The little muscles in my neck tightened, shooting pain into my skull. My brain couldn't stop going over the salespeople fighting about whom should get credit for a jewelry sale. If it wasn't the salespeople fighting, it was those few unrelenting customers making endless demands. Sometimes, I wanted out. Out of everything.

Agitated, I jumped up from my meditation spot and said, "So, what do you want for dinner?"

He asked, "Why don't you go and get us pasta from Giorgio's restaurant?"

That night I talked with God, the Divine Cosmos, "Dear Sweet Lord, if this relationship doesn't work out, could you please send me someone that understands my mystical side, someone who values harmony and doesn't want to argue all the time. Does anyone like that exist for me?"

CHAPTER TWENTY-EIGHT

Studying Esoteric Ways with Karl Wolf

A WEEK LATER ON JANUARY 9, 1989, Karl Wolfe happened into my boutique to buy a piece of jewelry for a friend. As I explained the healing qualities of the gemstones and the symbolism in the images of the Native American jewelry, he ventured to tell me about a class he would be teaching soon. I enjoyed talking with him, but his class seemed expensive, therefore I made an appointment with him so he could tell me more about it.

Karl and I met the next morning in the living room of his friend's home where the class would be held. It was sparsely furnished, classically elegant, and fresh-smelling. Karl told me about his life's experiences that led to him teaching about energy and self-awareness. Since I had been becoming more acutely aware of the energy and vibrations of people and things, I felt this might be a good class for me.

He told me how important the second chakra is for the union of Heaven and Earth energies. He demonstrated by speaking from his second chakra (located below the belly-button) and then from his mind. I noticed how his voice changed when he shifted back and forth from the different points of reference. Then I intuited why the energy of Tai Chi is built up at the second chakra. I realized that, for a short time now, I'd wanted to be finished with that chakra's energy. I only wanted to work with my heart, throat and crown chakra's, devaluing the second chakra's energy. Once again, I realized that all our energy centers needed to be in harmony and working together.

Suddenly thinking about Robert and my business, I experienced a deep sadness. I thought, *if only I could make some kind of internal shift, maybe then Robert's and my relationship would shift for the better.*

Observing me, Karl said, "Irene look around the room and see the objects in it. Become part of the environment. Notice what happens to your feeling."

I looked at Karl. I said, "The feeling dissipated. I remember doing a similar thing with my mom. She was feeling depressed and I had her look at a rose in my garden. I asked her to describe the color, and if she noticed how velvety it looked. I asked her, what did it smell like to her? She came out of herself. Noticing her shift, as a joke, she also asked me if I was some kind of psychologist?"

"Another good way to be with people is to keep *soft vision*," he continued, "which is basically the same as using our peripheral vision, keeping the environment in view when speaking with a person or a group of people. That way they don't feel so focused upon. It'll help your jewelry store sales."

"Castaneda talked about peripheral vision in his books," I responded, "as a way to be more fully aware of the environment. If you get soft enough you can almost see behind you. It's amazing how we easily forget awareness techniques if we don't develop them as a habit."

"That's why I teach a six-month class, so that you'll practice these techniques so that they become part of your character."

After spending one hour with Karl, I joined his class. I went back to work and practiced the second chakra talking and soft vision, making some easy sales. Talking from that area helped me connect easier with the client, somehow it took me out of my thinking mind and helped me to be more in the moment, and the soft vision helped me to be more present, making me appear softer than I would appear if I had only focused on the client. Class started that evening at 7 PM.

First nights of a new class always both excited me and intimidated me. When I arrived, most of the students were sitting in chairs arranged in a circle. A few people were getting themselves a cup of coffee. I had just helped myself to coffee, when Karl rang a tiny bell and asked us to please be seated. I ran over to the last vacant chair.

Karl had us introduce ourselves. A few ladies seemed like they would be interesting to know. The class was expensive, so most of the students were entrepreneurs seeking to improve themselves. He said that through our participation in his teachings, we would raise our self-awareness, and it would benefit our lives.

After that, he had us walk in different ways and at various speeds. As we walked, Karl pointed out to one person, Phil how his upper torso was leaning forward as he walked, emphasizing that his mind was leaning into the future too much and wasn't being in the present. Karl asked Phil to adjust himself and stand up straight when he walked.

Karl asked, "Does standing erect cause a shift in your thoughts, Phil?"

Phil said, "Yes, I was feeling anxious and thinking about something I need to do tomorrow. But, now that I'm walking erect I feel present in this room and class."

Karl had us walk some more. Then he pointed to Jennifer and asked, "Jennifer, what are your thoughts?"

Jennifer said, "I was thinking about an incident I had with my mom last week."

"Did you feel your torso leaning behind your legs as you walked?"

She said, "I did feel myself holding back, but I wasn't aware of my body showing it. I'll pay more attention."

Karl explained how just by taking the time to check in with observing our body position when we walked we could slow down, breath, and make our torso erect in alignment above our legs and shift us into the present moment, making us more conscious for the matters at hand. By being aware of our thoughts, we have the choice to shift them.

After the discussion, we walked around experimenting with our postures and observing our thoughts.

Next, Karl put on some flowing music and he had us all dancing, but we were to dance alone and not relate to anyone else. Then we were to dance with a partner and attempt to keep our energies in relationship. In the next experiment, we were to keep our energies focused at the second chakra while dancing, and observe if our thoughts dropped.

Afterwards, we took some time to share our thoughts and feelings about the experience. Most of us felt it was easier to dance alone. Some of the best ways to dance with the other person was to mimic their dance moves and flow into them. Then if we were lucky we could flow in and out with each other's moves and make a new dance. I knew a sales technique where we would imitate the client's positions in order to build rapport. This was a similar technique for gaining rapport with others we meet in everyday life.

Next, we each had to choose a Tarot card to contemplate for the following week. Fearing the worst card of the deck, I slowly pulled a card from the pile spread out on the wooden coffee table. I got the hangman card. My first thought was that I felt hung-up. Afraid of judgement, I get easily scared sharing my feelings in a new group.

However, as I looked at the card more closely I could see that the man was hanging upside down by one foot from a tree limb. He had a golden glow about his head, and looked peaceful, as if he were in a yoga pose. He also symbolized getting a different view of life. I thought, *Okay I get a whole week to look at this symbolic card*. We each shared what we thought of our chosen card.

Toward the end of the class, Karl had us meditate while listening to music. I asked myself: where did my fear of groups come from? Then I remembered my mother being beat up by another woman when I was three years old. I'd felt helpless and didn't know if I was next, but I didn't want to leave my mother.

That painful scene still evoked my emotions. We were a white minority living in an African American ghetto. A group of African Americans gathered, forming a tight circle around the two fighting women. The group yelled, "Kill her, kill her." Later in life, I had read that groups could take on their own pathological psychology. I had witnessed this group violence many times in the ghetto in my first nine years of life. Now I shivered and often cried when I saw it in movies. I always liked to sit near a door at concerts. I wiped the tears from my eyes, hoping no one noticed. I thought, *It would be nice to get over this fear*.

Once home, I taped my Tarot card on the bathroom mirror, where it would be seen often. Various types of Tarot cards had already been my habit for my daily guidance, and for helping me to balance my emotions. Through Tarot cards, the universe spoke to me in symbols, and helped me contemplate possible solutions for life's challenges.

Eyes shut, I pulled out the Hangman card from the *Motherpeace Round Tarot* deck by Vikki Noble, being surprised by the synchronicity. Swami Radha had recommended these cards for their creative, life-enhancing symbolism, finding them to be a more feminine spiritual deck. While reading about the Hangman card from the *Motherpeace* book, one interpretation said that the human gives up his attachment to his personality, turning more fully towards his soul or higher self. That to me seemed a great starting place and focus for this new class.

My work in this one night a week, self-awareness class with Dr. Karl Wolfe continued for a year. Through use of sound, dance, movement, tarot, video, dreams and journaling, we self-seekers sought self-awareness. I learned a lot about myself as well as about the minds, emotions, and hearts of the other participants. The class made me extremely aware of how my movements and gestures affected my psychology, as well as my physical being and vice versa. For instance, if I sat in a slumped depressed posture, I may have felt sad. If I changed my posture, sitting straighter with my head alert, much of the sadness dissipated.

Now as an adult, after practicing yoga and gaining detailed awareness of various body postures, I was realizing how empowering these positions could be. I had observed the blessing positions of the yogis, saints, and deities in paintings. When traveling, I often posed for photographs in the same pose as the statues and deities. I wondered, *What energy did these certain postures emanate?*

Also during this time, I believe, that the awareness work in Karl's classes, as well as practicing yoga and tai chi caused me to have an unusual experience. As I sat still one day, I felt a shaking in a small area in my body. Suddenly, I felt a great release of energy, and started crying. Just as quickly, a great joy filled my body.

From some past trauma, I innately knew that energy had been contained in that part of my body. Renewed energy flowed through my nerves and veins. It was revealing to know we could undo this blocked energy (illness). Even a simple, relaxing, freeform stretch dance had the power to release blocked energy.

Shortly after that experience, I read in a health magazine article that when people get shocked or traumatized, the emotional pain goes to a weakened part of the person's body and becomes locked in their cells and possibly into their DNA, where it festers and may eventually cause illness. I contemplated: what if, at a moment of emotional trauma or sadness, a person had enough awareness to see where this sadness was settling in his/her body. Then he/she could visualize the negative emotion radiating out and dissipating, cleansing oneself of it.

In Karl's class, I connected with a woman named Wendi Hill. As our friendship grew, Wendi and I shared conversations about astrology, philosophy, health, psychological issues, and our love of animals. Friends with whom I could share the deeper meanings of life gave me great joy. And it was often this kind of exploratory class where I met such wondrous friends. Paradoxically, little did I know, Karl's class was preparing me for losing a friend.

CHAPTER TWENTY-NINE

The Hero's Journey / Pivotal Dreams

"Follow your bliss and the universe will open doors for you where there were only walls."
— **Joseph Campbell**

JUST BEFORE MY 37TH BIRTHDAY in February 1989, I bought the videotapes of Robert Morris interviewing Joseph Campbell on his work with myths called "The Hero's Journey." That evening, Robert and I celebrated my birthday by watching the first few videos. Joseph said that in the dragon myths, slaying the dragon was symbolic to slaying your ego, opening up to your greater self. The act of slaying one's ego was a form of sacrifice. He talked also about the hero doing what he needs to do, what he knows innately to be true, regardless of society, and that it was only through this virtuous path that he might transcend himself, and contribute to the world.

Joseph Campbell's mythic stories influenced my dreams that night as well as future dreams. I dreamt that there were many people enjoying a leisurely day in a park. A baby was crawling on the grass, with no one nearby. I watched it from across the sidewalk. A crocodile moved toward the baby, preparing for his attack. A Divine Mother figure appeared, like an angel from the sky, pointed, and made the crocodile back away. The angel disappeared.

Then the crocodile walked towards me, backed away, and focused on the baby again. Determined, I ran to protect the baby, even if the crocodile might kill me. I ran toward the crocodile, and at that moment of self-sacrifice, Divine Mother reappeared and by just looking at the crocodile, forced it to swim away.

There are many levels on which to decipher a dream, but my main takeaway was that when one self-sacrifices for another, Divine Grace is present. A similar interpretation for the dream is where all the characters represented aspects of myself. The baby represented my new spiritual self, upon its path, and the crocodile represented my baser emotions and drives that could keep my spiritual self (the baby) from progressing. The rescuing woman, me, is the higher self that sees the need to sacrifice the desires of the lower self, the crocodile. And Divine Mother is the grace that is always ready to help our soul (the baby) to evolve.

In another dream, I was moving into a house previously owned by a couple that I'd liked. They left some objects behind and others for sale, some of which had value, but little meaning for me personally. In the dream, Robert helped me get rid of all the items. Once the house was emptied of all the items, I told Robert that I was so happy that that they were taking all this old stuff away, that the house felt like mine. To me, the house represented my body and the objects symbolized old habits that I still maintained, but those old habits didn't contribute to my clarity of mind or to my spirit's growth. It was a lesson in letting go.

One dream, I titled, "Free to Choose Oneness." In the first dream sequence, I was in a multi-storied building in a long hallway, much like when I was a child living in a ghetto. A man was attacking a lady and me. I told her that if we stuck together we could overpower him, which we did. The police took him away. To me this meant, I was no longer a poor helpless little girl. I now valued my feminine aspects, and would let those creative sides to powerfully unite.

The dream changed, and I was invited to be a star actor in a movie. It was a film where I had liked a male actor, following him around a party, sensing that he liked me too. The party ended and I found myself in bed with my ex-husband, but in a puritanical way, whereas we had no desire for sex, but we still cared for each other's well-being. The bed was a metaphor for creating things (like the jewelry business) in life together.

The doorbell rang. I ran down the stairs to open the door. The actor I liked, says, "I have a gift for you and good news. The critics loved your performance and the reviews were good." I reached up to give him a quick kiss, but the moment our lips met, it was a sensuous union, melting in each other's embrace. Once our lips had parted, I noticed a present wrapped in tissue paper with a note that read, "Poor, poor, Irene." He said, "You had looked that way earlier." He took back the note, crossed it out and wrote, "Light, light, Irene."

Looking into his smiling eyes, I said, "I'm not concerned about my weight, not like the other stars."

Leaning towards me, he whispered, "Think about it, the light. You have lightness of heart." His breath blew upon my neck, sending shivers down my spine.

Oh, I thought, *he was referring to my earlier condition in life, when he wrote poor, poor Irene…that I was still carrying an energy imprint of being poor and helpless.* "Should I open this little gift?"

"Sure!"

Upon opening the tissue paper, a beautiful diamond necklace sparkled. "Wow! Are the diamonds real?"

"I knew you wouldn't accept anything, but the *real*."

"This is so beautiful," I said. "But, I'm a bit confused. Is this a gift from you as a representative of the company, because of the film's success or because you like me?"

"What do you think?" He lowered his head, his lips kissing mine.

I wanted to make love with him, but all the moral issues bubbled up. I should know him better and experience being with him. Meanwhile, Robert, the man I live with in waking life, was standing nearby. Then this man's ex-wife walked by, saying hello. However, much to my surprise, everyone was emotionally neutral.

I thought, *I'm free to choose my own experiences.* So, I made passionate love with this man.

To me, this man represented my inner male self. This dream was teaching me that our perceptions of what we think that our loved ones and peers think about us, can keep our own inner male and female energies from uniting, and keep our soul from evolving.

The beginning part of the dream took me back to being the poor powerless little girl in the ghetto, that if I identified with it, it would keep me from being a star, a star in my own life, and like a star in the sky, symbolizing being connected to the heavens. And when he said, he knew I would only accept what was real, something having a real inherent value; it moved my heart because I had accepted that only our higher spirit represents any true reality, and daily life can be illusory.

Another dream was titled, "Inner and Outer Beauty." Sitting in a café in strange surroundings, a beautiful weightlifter lady sat at a table near me. I said, "I admire your beautiful body. I know how much discipline it takes to maintain and create a sculpted body."

She said, "You know, what I like about you is that each day you give me words of wisdom and I really value that."

From this dream, I was reminded of the importance of inner beauty and wisdom.

In still another dream, I was given the role of an actor again. Five men (could be symbolic of the five senses) interviewed me for a part, showing me the scripts. Not liking the scripts for being too violent and for having too much drama, I told the men, my acting would be great in some light comedy with a message. This dream made me laugh. I was always being reminded of the way to be.

"In the Moment of Self-Sacrifice

for Another Being

or for The Greater Good,

Divine Grace is There to Help You."

Irene Vincent

CHAPTER THIRTY

Swami Vishnudevanand Visits in May and Late July

EVEN BEFORE SWAMI VISHNUDEVANAND arrived from India, my mind filled with philosophical and spiritual questions. I'd already felt his presence. It had been agreed that swami would visit three weeks in May and then later in July. Carlos and I drove to the Los Angeles airport to pick him up. Carlos prepared Swami's favorite flat breads and a vegetable curry stew that would last three days. This stew and orange soda kept Guruji happy.

Even though, Robert agreed to and encouraged Swami's visits, he seemed on edge and wasn't very nice to him. He would often walk away when Swami asked him a question. He complained to me, saying, "Oh, he isn't that holy, he doesn't know so much."

He had similarly complained when his own teacher, Swami Radha, had visited. It was as though he felt in competition with them. Perhaps, he felt jealous that I loved these people so much. It was difficult for me to appease him, because I was going to keep inviting these wonderful spiritual people to our home.

Swami and I got along great. Each morning when I sat down for breakfast, he sat across from me at the table. He already knew the spiritual and philosophical thoughts in my mind, giving me a lecture on the subject. Sometimes he told me ancient spiritual stories with lessons.

I rarely spoke, because Guruji would say that he couldn't understand my heavy accent. I finally came to the conclusion that he just liked me to practice silence. As I spent more time with him, I realized we were developing a psychic rapport, which was good and bad.

One morning while I was eating my breakfast, I hadn't quite drunk enough coffee, and I was thinking about having made love with Robert the night before. Realizing that Guruji might be picking up my thoughts for the morning lecture, I chanted OM, OM, OM, over and over in my head to change my thoughts. Feeling embarrassed, I was almost sure that Guruji could see my red face.

In his heavy Indian accent that I somehow learned to decipher, Guruji said, "Oh Irene, the mind is such a monkey jumping from limb to limb. Eventually you'll get control over your thoughts." He chuckled and proceeded to tell me a story.

That evening when I got home from work, I noticed Guruji sitting in the backyard near the pool. I decided to test him to see if he could read my thoughts. Reaching down feeling the water, I read the pool's thermometer as ninety-seven degrees, and in my mind, I asked Guruji if he knew the pool's temperature. I stood up and looked at Guruji.

Waving his hand like so, so, he said, "Today was hot. Is ninety-seven degrees, something hot for water?"

Another time, I was sitting in a different room than Swami. I thought, *Guruji tells me stories; he tells me he is both a Jnana Yogi (yoga of the intellect) and a Hatha Yogi (yoga of the body), yet he hasn't taught me any asanas (yoga postures).*

Suddenly Guruji ran into the family room and said, "Irene, come outside and I'll teach you some asanas."

Surprised, I said, "Okay." I quickly followed him out into the backyard.

He began raising his shoulders up and down, demonstrating how to release tension. At 88 years old, he was giggling like a little kid. After he demonstrated a few more postures, he told me that he was a going to have his disciple, Carlos find me, one of his favorite books on the subject: *Yoga Self-Taught* by Andre' Van Lysebeth.

I planned for Guruji's lectures after asking him for a few titles. I would make a flyer and distribute it to metaphysical bookstores and community bulletin boards. I phoned everyone on our growing list of spiritual aspirants and acquaintances, inviting them to these lectures and the subsequent feast of vegetarian curry.

My colleagues at work, as well as some acquaintances, asked me, "Why are you inviting an old man from India to stay in your home?"

"It's such an incredible blessing to have such a beautiful spirit residing in my home," I replied. "When Guruji walks by me, waves of peace flow over me, causing me to feel relaxed and peaceful. When I sit down for my breakfast, he sits across from me at the table. He seems to know any spiritual or philosophical thoughts that I've been contemplating recently and he gives me a lecture on the subject. We go for a walk most evenings when I come home. Other aspirants are showing up to walk with him as well. These people have become special friends. Guruji laughs and giggles with me like a little child. He calls me his spiritual granddaughter."

CHAPTER THIRTY-ONE

Not So Easy, Along with Some Good

MORE AND MORE, Robert pursued arguing with me as a way of communication. He had mentioned after our past trip to Palenque, Mexico how much he wanted to go to Antigua, Mexico to study Spanish for a year. Then he could possibly come back and teach English to Spanish children. He really wasn't that enamored with his work in human resources. I knew that Swami Radha had told me that the one thing that inspired Robert at the ashram was to create and direct plays with the children.

Early on in our relationship, I told Robert that I didn't want to have children. He said that he didn't want children either. I explained to him that I felt everyone was my family in relationships; they were my parent, my sibling, and child, all at the same time. I felt motherly to everyone. If I ever felt I needed a child or to be around children, I would teach them art or some other activity. At that time, he went and got a vasectomy.

Sometimes I wondered if he had made the right choice for himself. I could feel his wanting to be in command of his own ship so to speak. Literally, too. We'd joined a sailing club. He'd had a cataract removed from one eye, and so at times still sported a black-pirate eye patch. At first, he would put it on as a joke and say he was captain of the ship and that he controlled everything when we were out at sea. I laughed, but I could see in his eyes that he was dead serious. I felt sad that he didn't see that he had a lot of choices in life. To me choice equaled a type of control.

Feeling an obligation to confirm his desire, I said, "Yes, Robert, you have the sailing knowledge, you are captain of the ship and you control things out here." I was embarrassed when he said that in front of friends that went sailing with us.

He continued to say that soon he'd be getting half of my savings and estate. On the other hand, I was more upset that he had paid back his mom all the money he'd borrowed from her, and yet he still didn't want to contribute to the household's monthly bills. He'd say, "You have to pay them anyway."

We had a lot of great times traveling together; he was definitely my adventure partner, especially to ancient ruins. This part of him I loved dearly. We also loved sharing a book by reading aloud to one another. Once, we had been reading, *Clan of the Cave Bear* by Jean M. Auel, and somehow the story influenced us. While we were making love, we were transported to an ancient time and were making love in a cave. When we had finished making love, we looked at each other and said, "Wow, I went somewhere else in time." After sharing details of the surroundings and the cave, we realized that we had been in the same dream-time. Experiences like this gave me a special feeling of connection to him.

However, sometimes it felt as though he was sabotaging the relationship. In my last neighborhood, my cats were outdoor cats. They mostly played on our house's one story roof, hiding behind the brick chimney; quickly jumping out at the sight of a bird, pouncing for it. Now, I had to protect them from coyotes and dogs in the new neighborhood. There weren't many fences built yet where the cats could jump behind for protection. In the new neighborhood, however, I felt guilty for taking away their freedom, making them indoor cats. Once in a while, I would take them on a leash for a walk with me outdoors.

Upon seeing the cats on leashes, my new neighbor, Akram asked, "How is it possible that your cats walk near you without protest? I've never seen such a thing."

I replied, "In my last neighborhood, when I went for short walks, I let them follow me. When they went astray, I called them back to my side or I fetched them and carried them until they got the idea that they had to stay near me. They don't seem to notice the leash very much."

"Amazing."

"Also, I had given them commands, like you would give to a dog. Now, I have to protect them against coyotes."

"We hear them howling during the full moon."

"I do, too," I said with a shudder. "Their yelping and screeching sounds are so eerie. I think it's when they catch a rabbit or some critter. I get shivers down my spine, even now just talking about it."

"That freaks me out, too. We'll have to build the stucco walls between our houses soon. That'll help protect them."

"Akram, time for lunch," Fatima, his wife called out in a sweet melodic voice.

"See you later."

"Bye."

Sometime later, there was an evening when, my cat Fang came into my bedroom and was meowing and hissing at me. Most of the time I put my Siamese cat, Coco and him in my art studio at night. However, that night Fang was extra aggressive against Coco, so I had to let him out of the room. Fang really wanted to go outside. He started to attack me. I looked him straight in the eye. He glared back at me. An ominous energy exchange occurred between us.

In a strong yet soft tone, I said to Fang, "My next cat is going to be gentle and more loving than you. I love you, but you are too mean." I picked up the angry cat, threw him outside the bedroom door and locked it. He banged and scratched against the door until he tired.

That night Robert came home late from an event at work. He forgot to be careful and Fang snuck right through his legs to freedom. During the night, I wasn't sure if I was dreaming or not, but I thought I had heard a screeching owl and a meowing cat. I got up several times to call Fang, but to no avail. In the morning, I noticed blood on the driveway across from my house. Hoping it wasn't his blood, I walked around the neighborhood showing my neighbors Fang's picture. Most of them recognized him. Apparently on the days that Fang snuck out, he had a system of visiting all the neighbors, especially those with cats. I called all the animal pounds near my home. I cried, reliving our last night's events. Heart broken, a part of me knew I would never see my furry friend again. And

I never did. A part of me questioned if Robert purposely let the cat sneak out. I still remembered how he let Purrsha out that day long ago, when I had told him that she looked sick, and please don't let her out. Yet, I knew mistakes happened, that I shouldn't dwell on those feelings. I could have locked him in another room.

Shortly after Fang disappeared, on July 7, 1989, I went to a ten-day Kalachakra Initiation with the Dalai Lama in Los Angeles, California. The chanting and guided prayers took me deeper into that spiritual chamber within myself. The huge semi-circular stadium was filled with padded seats and row after row of seekers. Looking around, emotions bubbled up from within me. I was grateful that so many people cared about becoming conscious and kind human beings. A tear gently fell.

At one point, the Dalai Lama talked about anger's energy and how an angry person shouting at another person is actually sending energy arrows of pain at that person. And, however, far you send that anger out; it comes back to you. It made sense to me because I felt pain when I yelled at another person.

One of the main lessons I had learned from my cat Fang, was that emotions traveled through the air, especially verbal emotions, like music set up its vibrations. One day when Robert yelled at me and I shouted back at him, Fang immediately meowed and hissed at our little cat, Purrsha. He attacked her.

At the time, Robert asked, "What's with the cats?"

I said, "They were fine, but now they are expressing our emotions. We need to process our feelings better and learn to communicate kindly, so we don't get to this level of yelling. We are putting vibrations of pain into the world when we are angry."

Robert calmed down and said, "Yeah, that was weird how Fang went from nice to mean."

I had thought about that emotion anger, because there was a psychological movement going on that proclaimed it was important to express your feelings. I didn't agree that it was okay to express mean feelings. It was important to realize that they were bubbling up inside, to feel them, and then question why, where, and who they came from. And find a way to calm down by transforming them through exercise, walking in nature, or some other way. Then work for a resolution.

My thoughts about Fang and anger faded as I heard the Dalai Lama speaking to the spiritual aspirants. For this initiation our attitude for wishing for Enlightenment was to bring ultimate happiness to all living beings. That thought filled me with joy.

Nevertheless, I felt overwhelmed by a sense of responsibility for helping to create world peace. World peace seemed huge and abstract. So much human suffering was caused by wars. This feeling for world peace was transforming into a caring for the souls of all beings on earth and even the souls of those who had passed. In the Divine Light Invocation, I had blessed all my teachers, past present and future and now this too took on new meaning. *Perhaps if I bless all the souls of beings throughout the world and universes, past, present and future, with light and love, it will actually bring peace to Earth. How can we pray, with our whole heart and soul to bring an essence of clarity and love to ourselves and others?*

My heart opening during the initiation made me want to overcome the sadness I felt at losing Fang. Maybe a new kitty would help. During my drive home from the initiation, I thought of names for my next cat. I wanted a name that would make me happy when I said it. Saying names such as

Delightful, Joy, Yeah, and Chocolate gave me good feelings. However, when I saw myself calling out the name Yahoo, I felt happy. Hence, his name was Yahoo and he appeared as an Abyssinian kitten.

Yahoo was an added joy. Being a little male cat, I wasn't quite sure how Coco, my blue-eyed Siamese, would respond to him. To my surprise, Coco became his mentor, teaching him how to open all the drawers and cupboard doors throughout the house. He showed Yahoo how to jump on the long-shaped door handles, swinging from them to open the room doors. Coco had a habit of sitting in the sink and trying to look up into the faucet to see where the water came from. Often, he got into funny positions. One day he coaxed the small kitten into the sink basin, tapping the faucet and the kitten's head, trying to get the kitten to look up it. *Are they actually communicating?* I wondered.

Yahoo seemed like a monkey, sitting on my shoulder and grabbing for the cantaloupe from my spoon while I was eating my breakfast. Soon I cut up little pieces of cantaloupe that he and Coco would slurp down. One day when I was slicing strawberries, I heard cat's feet romping across the upstairs floor, thumping down the stairs, and then suddenly Yahoo jumped on the counter and grabbed my strawberries. He liked fruit almost as much as he liked meat. He created new entertainment in our home, helping to distract me from the pain I was feeling from my relationship with Robert.

Now I Have It

Now I Don't

Let Go, Let Go-Oh

Now I Have It

Now I Don't

Let Go, Let Go-Oh

Let Go, Let Go, Let Go

A Releasing Chant by Irene Vincent

CHAPTER THIRTY-TWO

Swami Sahajananda Visits During the Breakup

JUST PAST THE SIX-YEAR MARK of our relationship, I told Robert that we should break up and that he should find a place to live. I offered to help him with his new first and last month's rent. Since he didn't like to help pay any of the bills, I thought if he took care of himself for a while and saw what it took, he'd appreciate me more. Then maybe we could get back together. He suggested we go to a therapist, but with a person of his choice. I agreed.

He chose a conventional Japanese psychologist, who saw us both together and then apart. Dr. Osaka said, "Irene, in order for this relationship to work, you need to marry Robert and give him half of what you own. A man needs to have his power."

"I'm not happy with how things are going," I said, "and I really don't see them changing just because I marry him."

"You're caught then in a catch 22, because he isn't going to change until he feels he's your financial equal."

"Well, I'll give this consideration. Thanks a lot." I thought, *This man is out of his mind. He comes from an old school of thought. There's no reason for me to come back.*

When I arrived home, I said, "Robert, we just aren't going to make it. This man comes from another culture. He might be supportive for you in us separating. I'll pay for you to see him a couple of more times so he can help you."

"Maybe we should try someone else. I'll call Donna and see if she knows someone. She wants us to stay together, so she won't be biased," he said.

"Okay."

Again we went together, and then each separately. After I finished my one on one with Dr. Tomas, he said, "Irene, it seems to me that you've made up your mind to separate. Now, it's about how to make it easy enough for you both to move on."

I didn't book another appointment.

Robert took me up on my offer to pay for him to get advice from the Japanese psychologist. He decided to look for a place to live, but stayed until the end of November.

Meanwhile, Swami Sahajananda visited in November. We chanted, sang spiritual songs, and meditated together each day. Twelve friends showed up for one of his lectures. On one of my days off work, Swami and I visited Yogananda's Ashram and Gardens in Encinitas, California. The garden was a beautiful serene place. We slowly walked around, pacing ourselves so we could savor the sweet energy there, like some people savor fine wine. We meditated together near the Koi Pond. It was easy for me to meditate in the company of Swami, attuning to his gentle vibration. I felt so blessed to have such a fine friend.

Even with the knowledge learned from my spiritual teachers and doing yoga and other spiritual practices, I still went through a time of having to constantly remind myself to straighten up and support my posture. My heart area kept feeling like it was collapsing, knowing my days with Robert were ending, and I would soon be thrown into the unknown. Swami being here helped me, but it felt awkward, since Robert was still here, and leaving soon.

Swami decided to give me a special guided meditation. He instructed, "Visualize a golden cross with a silk robe draped over it, blowing in the wind. Imagine, a golden disk with a six-sided star imprinted into it, the disk lying flat on the sand with a cool blue screen behind it. The cross is standing on a center point located in the six-sided star. A skull is hanging on top of the cross. Relax and stay in the silence."

Drifting into the silence, the longitudinal part of the cross became my spinal column, emanating light. The horizontal part became my arms. My muscles and flesh were as light as the flowing robe, blowing in a breeze. The skull reminded me of the impermanence of life, of death, and emptiness. The screen of blue symbolized the third eye, infinite intuition. And the six-sided star was the marriage of heaven and earth. It was interesting that a cross also meant being at a crossroads in life. The cross resting upon the six-sided star imprinted on the golden disk, meant the disk was support for choosing the higher path. Swami quietly whispered for me to come back into my body, which was relaxed, but in an erect posture.

After about eighteen days, Swami left. The tension between Robert and me took away some of the joy of Swami's visit. Swami had been hoping that he might be able to reconcile us.

That very next Sunday, Robert invited his mom and his niece, Kimmy to come visit. His mom started a political conversation as we walked on the beach. It was a perfect temperature, sun shining and the breeze blowing gently, the waves lightly crashing on the shore with their healing sounds. I just listened, even though I didn't agree with anything she said. I was proud of myself for avoiding a heated argument with her. Soon I wouldn't have to visit with her, yet a part of me felt a loss, a loss of what could have been.

When we got home, Robert suggested that he, Kimmy, and I soak in the Jacuzzi. Robert lured me into an argument over the respective benefits of tai chi versus karate. I had no idea how I let him pull me off my center. He was definitely a great tester for me. To help me recover from the emotional quarrel, I booked a massage for the next day.

That evening, after meditating, I opened to a random page in the book, *The Secret Oral Teachings in The Tibetan Buddhist Sects*, by Lama Yongden and Alexandra David-Neel, to where a footnote describes a disciple asking Buddha what his opinions were and the Buddha replied that he is free from all opinions. It was so appropriate for me to be reminded of that. In one of my past meditations I had heard the words, "God has no judgment, only men judge men. If we value our peace of mind, we don't need to have opinions. We can just see them as floating thoughts.

I cried, even though it was my choice to end the relationship. I needed clarity. I figured that I had better sign up for classes and get myself busy after work, at least a few nights a week. I would miss having yoga at the house.

While I was standing nearby, Robert called Swami Radha and talked with her about us breaking up. While I listened, he handed me the phone, saying, "Swami wants to talk with you."

Swami Radha told me I was welcome to visit her anytime at the ashram. She said that she wouldn't be able to stay at my house anymore because some of her past students were upset that I hadn't taken her six-month course and felt she was giving me too much of her time. They wanted her to go to their homes. I told her that I understood that she had only so much time, but it caused a deep sadness in me. She said that she was going to mail Robert and I a few Christmas presents early, so he could get his before he moved. I thanked her ahead of time. Swami Radha was so generous to her students and the people around her. She had previously told me that all the books she wrote helped to keep her financially independent, so she needn't use the ashram money for her personal use. I was hoping to connect with her again.

Those last few weeks, Robert slept on the couch and I slept upstairs. It was difficult. It's always hard losing a friend, especially since he said that he didn't want to stay in touch.

It felt strange being in my huge house all by myself, though sleeping downstairs on the couch took some of the fear away. After a week, I made my way back up to my bedroom. I decided to sleep, holding in my hand a favorite crystal which, to my surprise, actually grew hot from my body heat and acted like a bed warmer. A special dream came that was a precursor for how prominent the symbol of the eagle was to become in my dreams, in my visions.

I dreamt I was speaking on the phone with my beloved artist friend, Donna. While looking out an upstairs window, I saw three eagle dancer kachinas, (for the Hopi culture the kachina is a spirit of anything in the natural world and the cosmos). A male and female eagle kachina spread their wings wide-open, facing each other, standing close, moving in unison, in a circular mating dance. Another kachina stood by observing, witnessing the act, then joined in their dance.

Donna said, "Why are you so silent?"

I said, "I'm seeing a beautiful site outside my window. These three eagle kachinas are dancing. They look like colorful butterflies when they dance." I woke up inspired.

Fig. 80 Irene, Swami Sahajananda, and Robert sailing in Newport Harbor, CA

CHAPTER THIRTY-THREE

Oaxaca and the Spiritual Dilemma

WHILE AT WORK, I SEARCHED the cold steel safe for pieces of jewelry to replace the jewelry that had just been sold. I felt stabbing pains in my heart. Robert had written me a letter saying that he was now living in Mexico, and would soon be studying Spanish, just like he wanted. He asked me to meet with him in Oaxaca and travel to some ruins. This was the first I had heard from him, since we had broken up over a month ago. A part of me wanted to see him, perhaps to make amends of some kind, but I had no idea how he might treat me. It was brave and awesome that he followed his dreams of going to Mexico, studying Spanish, immersed in the culture. I wondered, *Who's going to be my traveling partner. Would I have to venture out on my own?*

Turning around, I asked my new employee, "Hey Vera what do you think of this necklace? It's left over from when we first bought the store years ago."

Vera was in deep concentration making jewelry tags for new pieces of jewelry. Looking up, she burst out laughing, barely able to speak. "A dog might wear it," she said in her sarcastic tone.

I laughed. "Maybe someone would buy it as a dog collar? I'm going to make a sign that says, Special Sale on Exclusive Sterling Silver and Turquoise Dog Collar, otherwise we are going to have to melt this piece. I'll show it to Ron and see what he thinks."

In a lightening flash, it dawned on me that Vera might make a good travel partner. She was a pretty good-natured person, but had a sarcastic wit, and sometimes used vulgar language. In the past, she had been one of our best customers, but times had changed, and she had recently asked Ron for a job. While visiting my home for Swami's lectures, Vera and I had a few spiritual conversations about our journey toward self-realization. Although she was about twenty years older than I, we had a lot in common talking about dreams, shamans, yogis and our mystical experiences.

Being a Tuesday, Ron was working in the store with me. I walked over to him and asked, "Is it possible for you to let Vera go on a vacation the same time as me? I haven't asked her, but I was thinking of going to Mexico for New Year's and I'm a little afraid of going there alone."

Ron froze for moment. "She's mainly a helper," he said finally, "not a full salesperson, so it'll be okay. Please don't travel there alone."

"Oh, and what do you think of this sign for this necklace? I laughed. "Vera said it was made for a dog."

Laughing, Ron said, "Yes, let's put it here on this necklace holder. I bet some extravagant lady will buy that gaudy necklace for her dog. A big dog will actually look stunning in it."

I walked into the backroom and said, "Vera, this New Year's I'm going on vacation to Oaxaca, Mexico to travel around the ruins there and then I want to go over to Palenque and try to see Bonampak. Would you like to go with me?"

"I'd love to go, but I don't think I have enough savings right now."

"How about if I pay ½ your plane fare, our tours, and the rooms. You pay for your meals, gifts, and incidentals?"

"It's sounding intriguing. Do you think Ron will let me take off at the same time as you?"

"I already asked him. There's just one more thing, that I don't know how to deal with."

"What's that?"

"My ex-boyfriend Robert wants me to meet up with him in Oaxaca and maybe go to some beaches. This is the first time he has contacted me since we broke up. I was thinking, I'll write him and let him know that you're traveling with me. We'll let him show us the Oaxaca area and then take off to Palenque. Would that be okay with you?"

"That'll work," Vera said. "I have some savings, so let's get planning."

Time passed quickly and we soon found ourselves having dinner with Robert in a lively square with different Mariachi bands playing mostly out-of-tune music. Even though Robert had received my letter saying that I wanted to go back to Palenque, he tried to persuade Vera and I to go to the coast with him, telling us stories of the beauty of the beaches and their cabanas. That evening, he walked us around the town, showing us an area behind a church covered in rubble.

Robert said, "This is where the locals hold their traditional "Breaking of Plates" ceremony. The people break their plates and pottery to mark the end of the current year's worries and to bring the dawn of a happy and prosperous New Year."

Shouting with loud enthusiasm, Vera said, "Sounds good to me. Where can we buy a plate?"

We found a vendor selling plates even though it was quite dark and late. We went back to the church and released our worries and made wishes.

That evening before we departed, Robert said, "I'll meet up with you after your tour tomorrow. I've already seen this area."

We both looked at him. "Are you sure?"

"Go rest at your hotel and when you get back, we can have dinner together at Café Carlitas."

After hugging Robert goodnight, we went to our room to sleep.

The next morning, Vera and I were having breakfast in the El Presidente Hotel in Oaxaca. Looking around at the unfamiliar scenery, I felt so excited about the new day's adventures. We took a bus tour, first seeing a two thousand-year-old Montezuma cypress tree called the Tule Tree, located on the grounds of a church in Santa María del Tule. It was more than 119 feet around and 116 feet high. Local legend stated that a priest of an Aztec storm god planted the tree over 1,400 years ago. Embodying a powerful presence and strength, the tree created a major home for hundreds of birds, tweeting their songs. I felt honored to stand near this tree, hoping to gain some of the ancient knowledge it had witnessed over its long time rooted in the earth.

Next we traveled to Mitla, located in the upper end of the Tlacolula Valley and, as the tour bus guide informed us, the second most important archeological site in the state of Oaxaca. It's known as the most important site of the Zapotec culture.

After getting off the bus, we were amazed by the elaborate mosaic fretwork and geometric designs covering tombs, panels, and walls. The tour guide, Carlos, told us that the mosaics were made with small, finely cut and polished stone pieces that had been fitted together without the use of mortar. I hadn't seen this type of stonework at any other sites.

Mitla was a main religious center. It's one of the pre-Columbian sites that represented the Mesoamerican belief that death was important, having been built as a gateway between the world of the living and the world of the dead.

Soon as we could ditch the guide, Vera and I went down into one of its tombs, where there was a wide column around which several myths abound, including greater fertility if you hug it. The tomb's energy was powerful, expanding my heart. After that, we went up into a building with four long narrow meditation rooms facing the four directions. Each room was covered in exquisite geometric carvings. The energy was extra powerful there, as well. Thankfully, I had some time alone to meditate. Then it was back on the bus to Oaxaca.

Arriving back at 2 PM, Vera and I had lunch in an outdoor café that overlooked a square where it was fun watching people bustling around, tending to chores. Then we hired a taxi to take us to more ruins, our first destination being Yagul, which was located halfway back to Mitla. Miquel the taxi driver told us that there were cliff paintings in Caballito Blanco, dating back to 3000 BC. Yagul was first occupied around 500–100 BC. Civic, residential, and ceremonial structures were built there around 500-700AD. The site functioned as the capital of a post classic city-state from 1250-1521AD. It was occupied at the time of the Spanish Conquest. He also told us that there were thirty tombs there, some with hieroglyphic inscriptions.

Vera looked at me with a funny expression, "Maybe we'll have contact with some ancient souls."

Smiling back, I said, "Yeah, that would be cool." Miguel was checking us out in the rear-view mirror, trying to see if we were serious.

At Yagul, Vera stayed behind to smoke a cigarette, chatting with Miguel. Eagerly, I trudged up the scattered stone path, with blinding sun rays bearing down, flying dust sticking to my sweaty skin. I was climbing to what looked like a high point at the ruins. An enticing path curved around a hillside, calling me. I stood there, wondering whether to go that way alone, when suddenly Vera appeared and said, "Let's see where it leads us."

Soon after, we realized we were on top of a tomb. I sat down and meditated for a while, having a vision of a Mayan God. After sitting nearby for a few minutes, Vera murmured she was off to explore some more. Walking out on a narrow ledge, I took in the vastness. Sparse green plants dotted the tan-hued land. Intense silence drowned out what was left of the chattering thoughts in my head, spiraling me into a state of nothingness.

Not knowing how many minutes had passed by, I was startled by a shouting voice, causing me to jump up. Vera was down by the cab, waving at me. I trotted carefully down the path. Miguel smiled and said, "You must have enjoyed yourself. You were gone quite a while."

"I'm in awe of the silence out here," I said. "Now I know why holy people go to the desert to meditate and have visions."

Miguel said, "It's good the sun is still up, because Monte Alban is a large pre-Columbian archaeological site with lots of carved images that you'll want to see. Let's go."

In the car, Miguel said, "Monte Alban is located on a low mountain range rising above a plain in the central part of the Valley of Oaxaca, only about 6 miles from Oaxaca City. Sometime around 800 BC, the Olmec immigrants actually leveled the mountaintop where they built tombs, a ball court and other buildings. In 300 BC, the Zapotecs took over Monte Alban, constructing pyramids, temples, and tombs. The Zapotecs had their own written language. They say they buried the site when they left it, but I think a giant dust storm covered everything and they left the place thinking God didn't smile on them anymore."

"That does seem more logical to me," I said.

Miguel continued, "It's said that, later on, their rivals the Mixtecs came and raided their tombs, unburying them, and then using them for their dead people. When the Aztecs arrived, it appeared to be just a hilltop to them."

As Miguel's taxi pulled in the Monte Alban's tourist parking lot, we could already see how impressive and immense the ruins were. Wanting to see as much as possible, Vera and I scurried around, first finding out the direction of the group of rock reliefs called the dancers. As we arrived there, a tour guide was telling a group of tourists that now they are now considered carvings of deformed people, showings abnormalities outside the entrance to an ancient hospital. As I knew that a lot of artists have distorted the human figure, to me they still looked like dancing figures. One figure did look like it was giving birth, but it looked more like a creation story.

Vera and I left there and started climbing up a pyramid, huffing and puffing, struggling to breath; we leaned against a wall.

"This is pretty impressive here," I said, "but I don't feel the spiritual energy I felt in the other places. Something feels off."

Vera said, "The feeling here is definitely different. Have you had enough?"

"Sure, let's go."

We hurried back into the cab, dozing off during the short ride back to Oaxaca. When the taxi was nearing our hotel, the sky turned to a dusky blue and the clouds lit with a rosy hue, inspiring me with a quiet happiness. Yet something about it felt foreboding.

I said to Vera, "I'm satisfied with a great day of exploration, but overwhelmed. I've barely enough energy left to eat. I hope Robert is okay. He was really pushing us into going to the coast."

"He'll be okay. After all, he was going to go there by himself anyway."

"That's right."

The taxi pulled up to our hotel. We bid our farewells to Miguel. On the door of our room was a folded note with Irene written on it, held up by an old rusty nail.

Reaching for it, I said, "That's weird, maybe there's a change of plans."

Vera looked at me shaking her head with downcast eyes, "No doubt, he was being a real pill last night."

I sobbed as I read the words, "Irene ... you are so controlling, and I had planned this trip for you." I thought, *How did he plan it for me when he didn't even ask what was important to me ahead of time?*

Continuing, it read, "I know how important you feel it is to end a relationship with a mutual sense of completion, love and forgiveness. I know you feel your soul needs this completion so that you aren't reincarnated or have to resolve these issues in another lifetime. So, I'm banishing you from my life and nothing can be resolved for you. I'm sending a copy of this letter to our friends, Donna and Swami Sahajananda, so they can see how horrible you are." I felt his anger blasting through the words.

He accused me of being selfish, controlling and of having no virtues what so ever. My stomach felt like it just got punched. Tears kept falling, as I wailed. Panicking and breathing irregularly, I struggled to steady my emotions.

I handed Vera the letter. Looking shocked, Vera asked, "Are you going to be okay?"

I managed to say, "Yes, I just need to release my hurt."

Suddenly, a realization stuck me. *It's my karma to forgive him and to feel complete within my soul. He didn't have control over my soul, or I over his.* Wiping my tears, I mustered up a half-hearted smile.

Surprised by my quick recovery, Vera said, "What do you want to do?"

"I want to burn his letter, then invoke the Divine Light, bless him, and forgive him and myself."

Vera said, "Let's light some sage and purify ourselves first."

After our burning and blessing ceremony, Vera said, "Do you want to pull a card from the *Motherpeace Tarot* deck?"

"Sure." I spread out the cards on the bed and felt for the one with the smoothest, silkiest energy.

I said, "It says, *sacred space*. Let me look it up in the book. It says, one must respect one's own sacred space and only invite worthy people into that space."

Laughing and nodding her head, Vera said, "That sounds about right. How about…after we have dinner tonight, we buy a few more plates and shatter them, drop these worries and start fresh?"

After eating dinner, we once again bought and smashed plates, laughing as we released our worries. We walked around town, taking in all the sounds, watching the colorful locals and the bustling tourists. When we arrived back at the hotel, I did some tai chi and yoga to relax my body. Reading some spiritual prayers from a favorite little book, I then drifted off to sleep. During the night, I woke up a few times feeling sad for what had occurred with Robert, but soon a peace washed over me and I fell back to sleep.

The next morning, Vera and I had a most wonderful buffet breakfast at the Presidente Hotel. Our dining table stood in an indoor atrium that overlooked a colorful garden, being a peaceful spot to start the day.

We bought an airplane ticket for Villahermosa, leaving at 8 PM that evening. After that, we went to the Rufino Tamayo Archeological Museum, seeing many clay artifacts from the ruins inspired me spiritually and creatively.

In another nearby museum, there was a Huichol exhibit. There were three artists, a husband, a wife and a man in his early thirties. Some prayer feathers caught Vera's attention, just as some colorful sculpted beaded art caught my eye.

Vera reached for some feathers and asked, "How much?"

The artist said, "They have no price."

I said, "Oh sorry, we didn't mean to touch your art. Smiling at the young man, I said, "We are both good spirits, so they're okay. Is this beaded bowl for sale?"

He said, "Yes, it's $40.00 US," warming up to us.

Feeling inclined, I said, "You know I had a dream in which an old Huichol shaman from your tribe came and healed me of a bad flu. I'm going to paint a painting of the dream. I feel a connection with your people." He smiled as I proceeded to tell him the dream.

I looked down, and a small beaded Jaguar head called my attention. I said, "Wow, this is so beautiful with its intricate patterns."

He said, "That is the only piece that I made and brought with me this trip. It's $20.00 if you want it."

"Yes, I love it. My spirit animal is the Jaguar."

After wrapping up my special new art piece, he handed Vera and I each a prayer feather.

I had a tiny bottle of sandalwood oil, which I gave to him.

Reaching out his hand, he said, "My name is Juan. In February, I'll be here studying with a healer for a month. You can join us if you like."

Trembling with joy at the thought of studying with a Huichol healer, but also recognizing all my obligations to my set life and business, I said, "My name is Irene. I would love to do that, but I have a business to run, and I don't think I could get away for a month, especially since I'm traveling right now. I sincerely thank you for the offer."

"Well, here is my card and phone number if there is a way you can show up," he said.

"Thanks for everything. Until later."

Vera and I had wanted feathers for our journey, and now we had them. Before we'd left on our trip, Vera and I had gone hiking and found some owl feathers. She taught me to pay attention to how light they were and to feel their vibration, their energy. They became a symbol for connecting with the divine cosmos.

During lunch, we read in a tour book about a place called Zaachila, where we could visit some tombs and ruins. The tour book stated that if you're lucky, you'll be there on a Thursday when the "man with the keys" shows up, and can let you into a special tomb.

"Hey Vera," I said, "It's Thursday. Want to go?"

"Hell yes," she said, "We're on a roll."

A taxi driver knew the tomb and drove us there. For a small price, the caretaker let us into the tomb. The symbolism of the artwork was amazing – there was an image of a turtle-bodied man flying through the air, a snake and a bird atop his head. There were four other figures. Carved owls stood on each side of the entrance. Sacred geometry decorated the beginning part of the tomb. The energy there felt very alive.

Fig. 81 The geometry of the ancient buildings at Mitla

Fig. 82 Tule Tree

Fig. 83 Stelae of dancing figures at Monte Alban

AWAKENING LOVE'S VIBRATIONS

Fig. 84 Irene and Vera at Monte Alban, Mexico

Fig. 85 Stele of creation image at Monte Alban, Mexico.

CHAPTER THIRTY-FOUR

Off to Villahermosa, Palenque, Bonampak, and Yaxchilan

ONCE BACK, WE ATE OUR DINNER and took our 8 PM plane trip to Villahermosa. In Villahermosa, a taxi driver found us a room at a Holiday Inn, where we were happy for some hot showers.

We got up early the next morning to go to the Parque Musé La Venta, to see the huge Olmec head sculptures. After paying our entry fee, we walked through a small zoo, finally seeing the huge carved images on the basalt stone. The volcanic rock sculptures were surrounded by lush tropical vegetation. One image looked like a man from a race that had beards, while a huge ten-foot head looked like possibly a sculpture of an African or Samoan, with a large nose and big lips. Another appeared more indigenous. Curiously, there was also a sculpture of a priest in a lotus posture. It's possible that ancient times saw far more transoceanic travel than many archeologists may assume.

We hurried through the park, because on this trip to Palenque, I was trying to fit in a trip to Bonampak, that I'd missed on an earlier trip. Making it back to the hotel just before 11 AM, we picked up our luggage.

We hired a taxi driver, Carlos to take us to Palenque. The stiff car seats caused us to feel the thumps of all the potholes. And when Carlos managed to steer around the holes, we were often facing head on traffic. Once in Palenque, he helped us book a hotel. Then Vera and I walked to town for a quick lunch.

By 2 PM we arrived at the Palenque ruins and hired a guide, Juan. He said, "I'll take you first to the Pyramid of Inscriptions to see Pakal's tomb. There aren't any tours right now, so you'll be able to take your time." We climbed the steep steps, carefully, most often on a side-stepping approach. Drenched in sweat, our clothes clung to our bodies. Breathing heavily, we finally made it to the top. Juan's hand shook as he inserted the key into the door lock to the tomb. "You go ahead," he said, "I'll wait here."

Vera and I looked at each other. Acting spooked, I said, "Why don't you want to go down? Is there something we should know?"

Catching on, Juan laughed, "Oh, the staircase is narrow, you turn a corner and go down some more stairs, then through a triangular opening. You'll see the tomb's lid. I'll call down if anyone else shows up."

Once in Pakal's tomb, I asked, "Do you think Pacal is in a space suit?"

Vera said, "It could be or it could show he's able to still get air even though he's dead or he's in some kind of ritualistic transition for his next life. Regardless, the sarcophagus lid is beautiful. Let's each put a hand on the wall and one on each other's heart, so we can tap a little more deeply into the energy."

"That sounds interesting," I said. After meditating a few minutes that way, we heard Juan yelling for us to make our way back up the stairs. We squeezed pass some people trying to make their way down.

Once up top, Vera and I were still contemplating when Juan said, "There is a hieroglyph date that equates to the year 692 AD, which is when they think this tomb was built. In 1949, when Mexican archeologist, Alberto Ruz discovered two large stone slabs with stone stoppers, realizing they must lead somewhere. Once the slab was lifted, he noticed a staircase filled with rubble. After a few years of clearing the stairways they noticed a stucco relief of a snake that traveled on the wall along the stairs which they believed symbolized the tomb's connection with the light and air above. At the base, they found a huge block of rock and destroyed it. Then they found a huge triangular stone and the skeletons of six youths. In June 1952, they turned open the triangular stone slab, revealing the crypt with its ten-foot-long-by-seven-foot-wide sarcophagus and its massive five-ton lid. Its weight is why the original remains here. Stucco sculptures of six standing and three seated priests, slightly larger than life, guarded the tomb. Pakal had on a Jade mosaic mask with shell and obsidian eyes. Jade wasn't usually found in this area, which created quite a stir. Also, pyramids in Mexico weren't known to have tombs in them until that time."

Pointing to the surrounding jungle, he continued, "This area of Mexico gets the most rainfall, causing the jungle to encroach quite fast over the ruins, to the point where they weren't visible. Today you can see around thirty-four structures in fifteen square miles. At one time, this stone city had been painted with brightly-colored pigments. Can you imagine its beauty?"

It was magnificent seeing the layout of the different pyramids from atop the Temple of Inscriptions, the tallest structure there.

Juan said, "Be sure to check out the palace. It has over twenty-five rooms. And the Temple of the Foliated Cross still has a large original panel. It's far back there, but it's worth seeing."

I said, "I've seen it and I want to see it again. I dreamt of it and it's actually what has spurred my desire to explore the Mayan ruins. By the way, we want to go see Bonampak. How can we get there?"

Juan said, "I'll give you an address to go to for a tour, but you'd better go there as soon as you're through here. Sometimes it takes days to get a tour."

Then Juan went with us to the Temple of the Sun. Inside was a relief that showed a priest on each side, holding up offerings to the sun. We bid Juan farewell. Then Vera and I meditated for a few minutes.

We picked up our pace as we made our way up the path to the Temple of the Foliated Cross. On the triptych panel, tall and short priests were worshiping a stylized cross that represented the god of corn. Cultivated corn helped create the rise of civilizations.

Vera said, "I'm going to explore a little of the jungle while you meditate. I'll meet you down over there."

"Okay, but stay near the edge, so you can hear me calling you."

As told in my dream, I placed my hands close to the imagery, hoping to know the wisdom of the Mayans. The energy felt so good there, so gentle and loving. After a few minutes, I climbed down the pyramid and found Vera in the jungle. She took me to a stream, where we did a blessing ritual.

After that we took a taxi ride to find the tour place. Once, there we were told we couldn't get an airplane, but we could get a two-day adventure package. It would be a four-hour van ride, then a six-hour jungle hike to Bonampak. It included a place to sleep, a morning car ride, and then an hour boat ride to the Yaxchilan ruins, and back to Palenque. I asked the guide, Victor, if I would be able to get vegetarian food.

He said, "The tour leaves at 8 AM. I'll pick you up at 6 AM at your hotel and you'll go with me to the farmer's market and pick out your vegetables. Then we'll pick Vera up and two young men who signed up. We also have rubber boots for rent, because the rain forest can be very muddy." So, Vera and I each chose a pair of boots.

Victor showed up at 6 AM to take me to the market. He told me to point at vegetables I liked to eat. I was amazed at the quantity he bought. Then we picked up Vera and the two men. One man was my age, around 37 years old and his friend seemed around 30 years old. During a two-hour bumpy ride, I half slept and half meditated, until we stopped for breakfast. Our new traveling companions, Andrew and Kurk sat with us at breakfast, and shared small talk. Kurk was bemoaning that his girlfriend had gotten sick and needed to stay behind.

Soon enough, we were bumping along the road again, laughing at the points where it was unbearable. Andrew had overheard Vera and I talking about how the energies at Palenque felt more loving and more present than at any of the other ruins we had visited.

He said, "I'm curious. How is it that you are able to feel these energies? I don't feel a thing that I'm aware of. Well maybe, sometimes a place does feel scary, but I think you are feeling something more."

Vera glanced at me. "Go for it."

I said, "First, I want to explain that we are all vibrating, everything is vibrating. If you look at part of a human being through an electron microscope, we are atoms: neutrons and protons vibrating in space. In a way, we are a microcosmic version of the universe. We can fine-tune our bodies to perceive and feel different energies/vibrations. On my path, as I practiced yoga, tai chi, meditation, and did shamanic journeying, it helped me to become more sensitive to the vibrations in my surroundings. And I could feel the energy in my body flow through me as I did these practices. Also, Vera taught me to feel the lightness of a feather and its vibration. I'm sure there are lots of ways I don't know about."

Andrew smiled, "I like your electron microscope story. That works well for me."

Kurk perked up. "Yeah, that actually made sense."

Victor pulled the van into a small muddy lot surrounded with jungle. After happily jumping out, we saw four distraught hikers covered in mud up to their knees, giving us concern.

I said, "How was your trip to Bonampak?"

One lady said, "It was too muddy, so we turned around after an hour."

Victor hopped out of the van. He said, "The road is too muddy to drive. Usually it takes six hours to walk roundtrip, but with predicted rain, it'll probably take you eight hours. Also it's noon and you need to be back before dark. Do you want to do it?"

Determined, I said, "I came all this way, I'm willing to tread through some mud. But you guys didn't bring boots. Will you be okay?"

Andrew said, "I'm willing."

Vera said, "Hell yes, I'm going."

Kurk said, "This is why we came, how bad could it be?"

Victor said, "Your jungle guide will be here any minute."

Armando, our jungle guide, was eleven years old, shorter than me. I'm thinking, *Oh no, he isn't going to protect us from a jaguar or an Anaconda. At least he has a machete."* I gave a quizzical; you got to be kidding look at Victor.

Victor said, "Armando knows the jungle well and will keep you on the path. Keep track of the time. Get out of there before nightfall."

In Spanish, Armando said, "Vamonos (let's go)."

After hiking for a half hour, Armando stopped and pointed at the ground, saying, "Muy bonito (very pretty)."

There were hundreds of large ants each carrying a freshly cut piece of leaf, each with its own pattern, and the group forming a walking mosaic, a piece of art. We each took a minute to view the scene. I appreciated Armando's innocent and loving perspective as he pointed out sites in the jungle. If I'd happened along on that ant scene by myself, I would've run for my life, having seen Tarzan jungle movies showing ants eating everything in their path, even people. This little boy made me feel safe. And also, the jungle's energy emanated a feeling of love, with its green healing light peeking through its leafy canopy.

The mud starting tugging more and more at our boots, as we trekked further into the jungle. More than once, Andrew had to stop to retrieve his hiking boot from the quagmire. Not more than two minutes after I whispered to Vera how I was so happy that we rented our knee-high boots, rain came down in buckets, mercilessly, drenching our bodies, filling our boots with water. All at once, the four of us stopped and looked up, obviously, never having been rained on that way before. We started laughing.

Mockingly, Kurk said, "How bad can it be?" We laughed and laughed, making it hard to walk. Armando blew his whistle, waving to us to keep moving.

After about two hours, we were wading in a stream and had to walk over eight tree trunks placed near each other that formed a bridge over a larger stream across a small ravine. It took three and a half hours to make it to Bonampak. The caretakers invited us into their home, a thatched roof hut with a dirt floor. They had a small wooden table and chairs, three hammocks, and a stove. The husband was weaving a hammock, while the wife was sorting rice and cooking. Two children were quietly playing.

Armando pulled our lunch out of a little backpack that he had been carrying. We had some sandwiches and sodas. The couple offered us some warm rice mixed with beans along with cups of steaming hot coffee, showing us that the water was purified and came from closed bottles. Chilled from the slight breeze that came with the rain, we were so happy for something hot to eat, and a caffeine boost for our trip back. The family was so gentle and loving towards each other that it really moved my heart. We ate quickly, knowing our time was limited.

Armando pointed to a small stone building on top of a pyramid. He said, "You only have half an hour, then we go."

After that arduous trek, I really had to push myself to climb the pyramid. But I knew there were famous painted murals inside three rooms in the building. The fresco paintings dated from 790 AD. They were painted in natural colors of indigo blue, azurite blue, red, sepia, yellow, mauve, green and purple. They were interesting and different in that the some of the figures seemed to be conversing with and looking at each other.

The first room showcased the consecration of a child, with the ruler's family enjoying a procession of dancers and music players. In the second room, the mural depicted a battle scene with torture and sacrifice of the captives. In the third room was a painting of a celebration of dancers with their headdresses with what were presumably royal woman being entertained. This was also the first time I saw captives depicted other than at Aztec ruins.

After a short reprieve, the rain started up again. We walked as fast as the mud and pools of water would let us. After three hours had passed, the jungle smudged out the light. We all hovered and kept pace with Armando. Howling, chirping, and croaking sounds filled the air. Soon we were in a line holding on to each other's wet shirts. Some fire fly reflections sparkled upon our watery path. My legs ached and I was chilled, trying real hard to believe that we were safe. Finally, Victor showed up with a huge flash light, saying, we only had about another twenty minutes more to go, which at that point seemed like an eternity.

The ordeal wasn't quite over. All of us were soaking wet for the drive to the hotel. The hotel turned out to be a metal building with four cots and no running water. They finally got a generator running, so we could turn on the one light bulb. Victor handed us each two sheets. He gave us a bucket of clean water from which I poured some on a towel to try to wash some of the mud off me. The others did the same. Then we all changed into dry clothes. Thank God, they told us to bring an extra set of clothes in case we got rained on.

Then Victor came and directed us to a house where dinner was served to us on the back patio. The cook brought out three dishes of mainly chicken with a few potatoes. Then he brought in my dish overflowing with vegetables. Everyone stared at my plate because it looked so colorful, so I shared some of my vegetables with them.

I did some yoga, tai chi, and prayers under the stars, praying that my body would be able to walk the next day. To fight off the chill, we slept in our clothes.

The next morning, we had an hour bumpy ride to get to a restaurant for breakfast. Then it was another half hour to a town where we took a long, canoe-like boat ride for an hour to the Yaxchilan ruins. On the way, Victor gave us a bit of the history.

"Yaxchilan's original name was Pá Chan meaning "cleft or (broken) sky." It has many carved stele, lintels, altars, bas-reliefs, and painted murals that reveal its history, showing the ruler's time lines, and their various important captives. Many of the lintels that give the history were carved around 740 AD. Yaxchilan was a warring and domineering power along the Usumacinta River.

Bonampak was only about thirteen miles away. Yaxchilan fought with it quite often. Yaxchilan warred with Palenque in 654 AD."

My mind trailed off with that bit of information upsetting me. It really broke my bubble of the Mayans living in a state of peace. Although, I still felt that Palenque was more like a temple village or monastery.

Victor, abruptly stopped speaking and then pointed towards the shore. "Look…a crocodile is crawling up the river bank. Stay away from the river's edge."

Shortly thereafter, the boat pulled on to the shore. Victor pointed out the trail, saying he was staying at the boat, and that we should return in an hour.

I was also on high alert as we hiked through the jungle up to the ruins, looking around me for crocodiles. The roaring from the howling monkeys still sent shivers down my spine. My tired mind, filling with fears, was finally alleviated when I saw huge tree roots, standing high, twirling and projecting out from giant tree trunks. I stood staring at trees while Vera and the men headed into the ruins. The energy felt very powerful. The trees were so large and beautiful. There was one tree that seemed almost as huge as the Tule tree. Its roots spiraled around the tree's base. I meditated and said some prayers while circumventing the tree. Vera saw me and joined me in this spontaneous ritual.

Then we explored the ruins for half an hour and headed back to the boat early. Kirk and Andrew were already there waiting to head back to Palenque. Laughing, I said, "I thought we would be the first ones back."

Kurk said, "You two are troupers. We're amazed at how cheerful you kept throughout the ordeal, especially last night in the jungle."

Andrew added, "We'd like to exchange addresses, to keep in touch and share pictures. If that's okay."

"That's a great idea," Vera chirped. "And by the way, in the dark jungle, we were scared shitless."

Fig. 86 Irene and Vera are standing on top of the Temple of Inscriptions, Palenque, Mexico.

Fig. 87 Pakal's tomb, Palenque

Fig. 88 Crossing the log bridge to Bonampak, Mexico

Fig. 89 Irene stuck in the mud on the way to Bonampak ruins.

AWAKENING LOVE'S VIBRATIONS

Fig. 90 Irene drenched up in the doorway of the pyramid in Bonampak

Fig. 91 Stele of slave taken prisoner at Bonampak.

CHAPTER THIRTY-FIVE

The Phoenix: Bird and Snake Singing to the Stars

*I*T TOOK A WHILE TO RECOVER, handling all the work that piled up at my business and the personal stuff that one has to take care of when one gets back from a trip. But soon, I had a day off in which I could relax. And my place to do that was in Laguna Beach, at Café Zinc, where I might, perchance, meet up with a friend from the art school.

I was walking toward Café Zinc for lunch, when I saw my artist friend, who had also been my drawing teacher, Artemio Sepulveda. He was crossing the street, walking toward the café.

I waved my arms and yelled, "Artemio!" as I ran towards him. We embraced.

We had lunch and coffee together, sharing what we each had been up to. Artemio had rented a small studio nearby and a few artists were coming to figure draw with him.

I said, "Count me in Artemio. I love to draw while in the presence of your enthusiasm, seeing your passion flow through your charcoal onto the paper. I still remember when you were painting that mural at the beach. The paint just dripped off your brush, magically forming anatomically beautiful feet in a few seconds."

Smiling for a moment, I continued, "A while ago you told me how the Mexican artists had experimented with creating unique textures. You mentioned about piling paint on the canvas and setting it on fire. I'd like to do that. Is there somewhere around here where we could make a fire and it's safe?"

"Actually, Irene," he said, "I'd like to start a painting with that technique. Behind my studio is a cement sidewalk that's next to a creek. Plus, for extra safety, we can have a couple buckets of water. Next Wednesday after the class, bring a few pieces of loose canvas and your paints."

I was excited beyond measure. Burning up paint on a canvas seemed so alchemical.

Finally, Wednesday came. Artemio and I went behind his studio next to the creek. He had two buckets of water and a bucket of dirty beach sand. I laid a piece of heavy canvas on the ground. The blowing breeze moved it around, getting creative itself. Scanning the area, I found some rocks to hold my canvas to the ground.

"Irene, choose your colors and pile the paint on thick. Watch me for a minute. Then put paint on the canvas. We're setting the paint on fire in order to create unusual textures. We need to be careful not to set the canvas on fire, but if the canvas does burn in areas, we could glue it onto another."

Piling gobs of paint onto the canvas and moving it around with sticks and the ends of my brushes using flowing gestures, I asked, "Is this enough paint?"

"Use more." Artemio replied.

"Is this paint still going to stick to the canvas after it burns?"

"Don't worry, we can always paint with medium over it and it will hold it to the canvas."

With anticipation, I watched as Artemio scattered a few twigs over his work. Then he dribbled a bit of liter fluid and set it on fire. The paint bubbled and swirled.

"Ok, it's your turn. Make some magic," he laughed.

His eyes sparkled when he laughed. I thought about how passion for creating art, dance, and music could be so exhilarating. As long as one can still function in everyday life, creating art has to be one of the best obsessions a person can have.

As I lit my paint on fire, the flames swirled and danced around the canvas. I laughed and twirled around, dancing with the flames.

Artemio handed me some sand, "Quickly, throw some sand around your piece so you can have some of the quartz embedded into your paint."

Smiling as he watched me, he handed me a thick rag. "Here, use this and put out the fire now."

"Look Artemio, I see a bird that looks like the Quetzal bird. It's the bird that symbolizes freedom and liberation. How cool is that? Do you see it?"

"Yes! And I also see a snake."

"Oh, I see it, too. I'll have to start working on this painting, soon. This was really fun. Thanks so much."

"Hey, de nada. We had better clean up and get going."

I took my unfinished painting home and tacked it to the wall. It was my habit to sit and contemplate the image. As I looked at the image of the bird and snake, I knew that birds ate snakes and snakes ate birds. I thought about my monotype "Some Enchanted Meeting." However, in this painting, the bird is holding the snake, so I had to make sure the bird didn't look like he was eating the snake. I wondered, how do I show the two opposites in the sky in an action of unity? I thought about the Mexican Quetzalcoatl snake with the feathers on his head symbolizing his ability to fly, as well as his spiritual origin. I knew about the Quetzal bird representing freedom and liberation, since it was known not to live in captivity and would often kill itself if caught. Long spiraling tail feathers, a feature of the Quetzal, was already appearing.

The myth of the Phoenix rising from its ashes seemed important for me to read about, since my image of a bird had appeared out of fire and ashes. I read that after the Phoenix lived a thousand years, she built a nest of twigs. She added incenses, breathed in the aromas, and then the nest ignited. In the all-consuming flames, the bird and nest were reduced to ashes. Out of these ashes, some say, after three days a newborn Phoenix arose. The new Phoenix embalmed her ashes with myrrh in an egg. Then she flew and deposited the egg in the Egyptian City of Heliopolis (Sun-City). This resurrection story implies the Phoenix's immortality. The sun often symbolizes spirit: after rebirth, the bird is immediately reconnecting with spirit.

In myths, the Phoenix was often depicted as red and gold in color, so I decided to paint the essence of those myths combined with my own experience of the spiritual process. I used reds, blues, deep purples and gold colors for the bird and snake. For me the red symbolized fire, passion and earth. The blues depicted the sky, water, and heaven. The deep purples represented spirituality, royalty, and deep space. The golden colors meant spiritual energy and blessings, that which is most valuable. Together the colors form the union of Heaven and Earth.

The snake shedding its skin signified transformation. And because a snake often slithers along the ground, it represents the earth.

I painted long head-feathers on the bird to show its power for *drawing-in* spiritual energy. The bird, a being of the sky, is the Heavens. Once more, I have the marriage of Heaven and the Earth, or the union of opposites.

Near its head, I decorated the snake with seven red diamond shapes that symbolize ether and Heaven, with circles inside them to signify eternity. These seven symbols painted on the snake show the seven chakras, the subtle energy centers in the human body. The snake with the chakras then took on Kundalini energy, the awakening of the spiritual centers.

Both the bird's tail and the snake's tail are spiraled, showing their spiritual energy and their connection to ancient cultures. The bird and snake with raised heads look as if they are singing. The golden spheres represent their song to the stars.

To symbolize my devotion to the Heavens, I put down in the left corner the golden outline of a triangle with a golden mark in the center. As I worked on the piece, I added sand to flow with the shapes of the feathers and brushstrokes. The bird and snake were painted as if hovering or floating in unison in the sky.

I became aware that most of my paintings had the theme of the "alchemical marriage," a blending of opposites, the Sacred Marriage of Heaven and Earth.

My paintings, contemplations, daily life, and dreamtime all comingled connecting me with the heavens in some mysterious way. These dreams and merging of realities were preparing me for powerful beings I was yet to meet and for the incredible mystical experiences forming in the ethers, waiting to enter my consciousness, pushing my perceptions of reality beyond my vivid imagination.

AWAKENING LOVE'S VIBRATIONS

Fig. 92 Irene Vincent, *Spirit Bird & Snake Singing to the Stars*, 60"H x 40"W
Oil is painted over sand and acrylic on canvas. It was mounted and repainted in 2007.

Third Book & Epilogue

AFTER WALKING UP THREE stone-covered wide stairs, I stood on the landing and searched in my purse for keys. A naturally occurring image of Buddha on a large rock graced the entry's left side. It reminded me to honor spirit before entering the house. Just as I was about to open the door, I turned around and looked longingly up at the stars. Dressed in long orange robes, Swami Vishnudevanand stood on the side walk below, waiting for me to open the door.

Bubbling with excitement, I said, "Oh, what a beautiful night Guruji. The stars are so bright."

Guruji giggled and said, "The universe has no secrets. It reveals all its knowledge, all its wisdom. You just need to be receptive to it." *Well that blew my mind open.*

Almost every time Guruji spoke to me, his words were not only food for thought, they guided and opened my mind, heart and soul to experience my higher self.

Standing silent for a moment, smiling at Guruji, I turned and opened the door. Guruji followed me inside, chanting, "Hari OM, Hari OM, Hari Om Tat Sat." Then he slapped me gently on my back and said, "May you be blessed to live a long spiritual life. May you live to be a hundred years old."

After he had slapped my back, this beautiful peaceful energy traveled up my spine and filled my body with a bliss.

Still in process, Book Three of my *Spiritual Trilogy* has the working title, *Delving Deep, Reaching High*, spanning the years 1990-2002. In this adventure-filled memoir, I share my deepening mystical experiences, insights of my teachers, psychic episodes, sacred travels, dreams, visions, and art. Not always sure about what was happening to me, I held an open mind, contemplated these experiences, read many books, and questioned spiritual teachers. You will discover some of the experiences you may encounter while on your spiritual path as I shed light upon mine. You will discover ways to navigate these realms.

During this period, I continued to spend cherished time with Swami Vishnudevanand and Swami Sahajananda along with meeting and being initiated by more teachers. Also, I met a gentle loving yogi, Nandu Menon and he became my husband. He taught hatha yoga, meditation, ancient Sanskrit, and pujas from our home. We shared our mystical experiences and dreams. Soon, I taught hatha yoga.

Also, I studied different branches of yoga with Steve Sadleir who had started Self Awareness Institute (SAI) in Laguna Beach, California. Because of Steve's sponsoring of yogis, I met and received an initiation from Shri Shri Shri Shivabalayogi that sent me into states of bliss and into automatic meditation whenever I sat still. Then an initiation from Yogiraj Vethathiri Maharishi and his form of Sky Yoga Meditation, helped me to gain some control over the bouts of automatic meditation. Simultaneously, I met Usha Harding, who's dream was to build a Kali Temple in Laguna Beach, California. She became a powerful part of our spiritual community.

My friend Vera continued to be a shaman mentor and traveling companion. We traveled to Oak Creek Canyon in Sedona and Canyon de Chelly in 1990. In Canyon de Chelly, I had a lucid dream vision, experiencing the great *Oneness of the Universe* that transformed my spirit. This experience inspired me to paint *Divine Ecstasy*.

Next, Vera and I traveled to Acoma Pueblo, Mesa Verde, and Chaco Canyon. Also in 1991, Vera and I took a 11:11 psychic tour to Egypt, where we were initiated at different temples along the Nile, having psychic experiences. After the Temple, that represented the heart chakra, while having a flu-induced fever, Christ along with angels showed up in a dream, initiated me and healed me.

In 1993, Nandu and I traveled to India, adventures abounding. In 1995, we traveled to museums and ancient Goddess sites in England. In 1996, we traveled to the jungles and volcanoes of Costa Rica. In 1997, we moved to New Mexico and then moved back to California in 1998.

Meanwhile, from 1990 forward, I avidly studied astrology, especially with Laura DesJardins. I traveled to many astrology conventions, studying with international astrologers. I gave readings, along with healings, and inspired clients to move forward with their talents.

Life also threw a number of challenges. Our jewelry store's retiring manager sabotaged it causing most of the employees to quit at the same time. I suffered from a frozen shoulder for a year and half and couldn't paint. Most of my beloved spiritual teachers died. To add to it all, I had an old chronic sickness return, but after months of pain a healer healed me. For a year, I studied healing with him, but then he almost died from a car accident.

What I learned was that when the outside world challenges us, if we have an inner happiness, and know ways to nurture it, we are empowered to live this life to its fullest, benefitting all peoples. And after discovering some of the ways to maintain inner peace and happiness, I hope you'll be inspired to continue your spiritual journey. So much love and in deep peace, Irene.

❖❖❖

Since those adventures, in 2002, in Austria I studied an egg tempera and oil painting technique that gave me dreams of painting with white light. It's an old master technique that creates luminosity in paintings not easily attained by other methods. After that, I traveled to various countries wherever Philip Rubinov-Jacobson taught the course. I continue to study and paint with this special technique and now teach it. Through Philip and others, I have connected with the visionary art community.

I find joy in writing, painting, dream journaling, traveling, hiking, doing yoga, meditating, and contemplating. I teach painting classes in intuitive and experimental painting methods using both oils and acrylics. And I offer *Art, Dreams and Visions* workshops and astrological readings.

After moving twice in Southern California in 2013, I moved to Port Townsend, Washington in 2014. Its spacious nature called to my spirit. In 2016, for four months, I opened Irene Vincent Visionary Art Gallery, introducing my art to the public. *Awakening Love's Vibrations* was finished here.

The peaceful environment helped deepen my spiritual disciplines. As much as I dislike the challenges of moving, I'm feeling the call to move again. A nomadic way of life seems to be part of my destiny. Moving and traveling keeps me in touch with what is going on in the world.

❖❖❖

After enjoying my book, please write a review on my Amazon page or on the site you had purchased it, so you can inspire others and let them know how it benefitted you, what insights you may have received, and what you enjoyed about it. I deeply appreciate it.

About the Author

Fig. 93 Irene Vincent, Photo by Jesi Silveria

Art Education:

B.F.A. Florida International University, Miami, Florida, 1977

Major: Painting, Drawing; Minor: Jewelry

Laguna Beach School of Art, Laguna Beach, California, 1979 – 1981

Figure Drawing with Artemio Sepulveda, 1979 – 1983

Performance Art with Tom Stanton, 1982 and with Valerie Bechtol, 1983

Studied Misché Technique with Prof. Philip Rubinov-Jacobson in Europe: 2002, 2003, 2004, 2005 etc.

Studied Old Master/Magical Realism with Robert Venosa and Martina Hoffmann, 2006.

I have been teaching painting classes that open up the imagination and tap into spirit and intuition from 2000 to the present.

Scholarships, Awards, Society Memberships & Activities:

Fine Arts Tuition Merit Scholarship, FIU, Miami, Florida, 1976

Excellence in Art Award, FIU, Miami, Florida, 1977

Scholarship Award, Figure Drawing, Laguna Beach School of Art, CA, 1979

Woman Artists It's Time, Miami, Florida. Membership 1975 – 1977

Participated in Hanging Shows for Women Artists It's Time

Student Association for Art, Florida International University, Miami, Florida, 1976

Participated in Hanging Student Shows, 1976 and 1977

C.G. Jung Club of Orange County, CA 1984 to 1987

Jungian Dream Analysis Study Group, CA 1984 – 1986

Orange County Center for Contemporary Art, CA (OCCCA) 1985 to 1987

AWAKENING LOVE'S VIBRATIONS

OCCCA/Director of Exhibitions, 1986-1987

The Inside Edge, CA (New Age breakfast lecture club) 1986

Honorable Mention - Cash Award for "Cat Man" sculpture, Irvine Art Center, CA, 1988

I personally studied with and had initiations from, and had yogis stay in my home: Swami Sivananda Radha, Swami Sahajananda, Swami Shantanand, Swami Vishnudevanand, Shri Shri Shri Shivabalayogi, Maharishi Vetarthri, etc. I had Initiations by the Dalai Lama. 1985-1998.

I was a member of SAI (Self Awareness Institute) led by Steve Sadlier and received several certificates of completion in the various branches of yoga. 1989 – 1992.

Studied ancient cultures, visited ancient sites and studied ancient symbolism, art and spirituality, 1988 to present.

Studied Astrology since 1990, member of AFA (American Federation of Astrologers) 1992 to 1994 and a member of SCAN (Southern CA Astrological Network) 1990 to 2014.

I have been a member of "Light Bearers" an Orange County Branch, 2008 to 2011.

Ron Figueroa and I started a MeetUp Group called CARMA – Center for Awareness, Releasing, Manifesting, and Awakening. "Healing occurs when we combine our energies and open our hearts to the Universe." Orange County, CA, 2011 to 2013.

Member of Greater Los Angeles Writers Society 2011 – 2014
Joined Toastmasters an International Speaking Club in 2013.

Publications:

The Miami Art Scene, June 12, 1976
OCCCA "State of The Art Catalog" 1985
The Irvine World News, July 17, 1986
Art Scene California, Vol. 6, No.5, January 1987
Art Speak - June 16, 1987, New York City
Viechtach Daily Newspaper Bavaria, Germany: July 2004
Eyes of the Soul by Philip Rubinov-Jacobson, forthcoming
Visionary Art Yearbook, 2010
Revealing – The Evolution of an Artist's Soul, by Irene Vincent, 2012
Dream Wheels, by Della Burford, 2013
PT Leader Daily News, "'Happy Realities' at Irene Vincent's Visionary Gallery" by Robin Dudley, Port Townsend, WA, June1, 2016
Imagination Reigns, by Della Burford, 2017

Book Cover Art by Irene Vincent:

Kali's Odiyya by Amarananda Bhairavan published 2000
Medicine of Light by Amarananda Bhairavan published 2007
Love Belongs to Those Who Do the Feeling by Judy Grahn published 2008
To Save a Dying Planet by Ron Figueroa published 2012, (Art and Cover Design)
Revealing – The Evolution of an Artist's Soul by Irene Vincent, published 2012

Group Exhibitions:

Miami Art Center - Miami, Florida, 1975 (Juried)
Women Artists It's Time Annual Show - Miami, Florida, 1975
Florida International University Student Shows - Miami, Florida, 1974 – 76
Coconut Grove House Gallery - Coconut Grove, Florida, 1976 (Juried)
Coconut Grove House Gallery - Coconut Grove, Florida, 1977
Juried by Marilyn Schmidt, Ph.D. and Arlene Olson, Ph.D.
Stanford Galleries - Baltimore, Maryland, 1981
Southwestern College, Chula Vista, Ca 1984, Juried by Michael Schnorr
OCCCA Membership Show, 1985
Spectrum Gallery, San Diego, CA, 1987
Amos Eno Gallery, New York City, New York, 1987
Irvine Art Center, Ca. Juried by Dori Fritzgerld, 1988
Fact Gallery, Laguna Beach, CA: Oct. 1994
Concordia University, Irvine, Ca, 1994
Viechtach Gallery, Viechtach, Bavaria, Germany, 2004
Plein Air Art Show, Giverny, France: July 2006
Magical Realists Show, Cadaques, Spain: August 2006
The Space Gallery, Eureka Springs, AK: May 2008
Sandstone Gallery, Laguna Beach, CA: June 2008
By 55 The OC Artist's Co-Op, Santa Ana, CA, July – December 2008
World Art Gallery, Ladera Ranch, CA, Nov - December 2008
Beauty and The Brush Gallery, Laguna Beach, CA, October - December 2009
Festival of Goddesses, Laguna Beach, CA, April 2011
School of Multidimensional Healing Arts and Sciences, Costa Mesa, CA, 2011 to 2017
Impact Health & Wellness Center, Costa Mesa, CA, July – October 2012 – 2013
Transformations, Long Beach, CA, January 2013 to 2017
Karja Wyan Art Space Gallery, Penestanen, Ubud, Bali, Indonesia February 2014
Karja Wyan Art Space Gallery, Penestanen, Ubud, Bali, Indonesia February 2017
Atman Nurturing Kafe, Ubud, Bali, Indonesia, February, 2017

AWAKENING LOVE'S VIBRATIONS

One Person Exhibitions:

Irvine Fine Arts Center, Irvine, CA, Portfolio Gallery 1987
Orange County Center for Contemporary Art, CA, 1987
30-Year Retrospect Show, Laguna Niguel, CA, 2007
School of Multidimensional Healing Arts and Sciences, Costa Mesa, CA, 2011-2016
Impact Health & Wellness Center, Costa Mesa, CA, July – October 2012 - 2013
Irene Vincent Visionary Art Gallery, Port Townsend, WA, May 1 – August 30, 2016

Irene's Sites and Online Sites:

Mystical, Visionary, and Surreal Art by Irene Vincent: http://www.irenevincent.com
Yessy: http://www.yessy.com/ivincent108
Deviant Art: http://ivincent108.deviantart.com   Features Irene's political prints.
Irene Vincent YouTube Channel: https://www.youtube.com/user/artistvincent
Facebook: https://www.facebook.com/artist.irene.vincent
Follow Irene on Twitter: https://twitter.com/#!/IreneVincent
Irene's Blog: http://irenesmysticalmoments.blogspot.com/
Society for the Art of Imagination: We wish to foster the resurgence of interest in imaginative and sacred art and make this art accessible to all.
ARTslant   Los Angeles - Online Gallery of Metro Area.
Architects of a New Dawn - Their Mission Statement -"A site to inspire, uplift, engage, and transform the global community through music and positive media content. To help bring about a world where we choose peace over conflict and love over fear.

Travel Experience:

Visited museums in Belgium, Netherlands, Germany, Switzerland, Italy and France in 1974
Visited museums in New York City and in Athens, Greece, 1975 and 1976
Five-day excursions to New York City visiting artists, Museums, and galleries 1974, 1975, and 1976
Trips to Jamaica 1977, Hawaii 1978, Tahiti 1979, New York City, 1980

From 1977-2017, in California, I often went to MOCA, LACMA, The Hammer Art Museum, and The Getty Museum in LA, visited the de Young Museum and The Modern Art in San Francisco. I visited OCCCA in Newport Beach, The Laguna Beach Art Museum, and the Pasadena Art Museum.

Trip to Mexico City and the Yucatan peninsula visiting Museums and Mayan Archeological Sites 1984
Trip to New York City, Rochester, New York and Toronto, Canada, 1984
Trip to Vancouver, Victoria, and British Columbia, Canada, 1985
Trip to Bangkok and Chiang Mai, Thailand and New York City, 1986
Trip to visit Mayan Ruins of Tikal in Guatemala and Belize, 1987
Trip to New York City, 1987

Trip to Lima, Cuzco, Machu Picchu & Nazca Lines in Peru, and La Paz, Bolivia, 1988

Trip to Native American Ruins, Southwest, USA, 1988

Trip to Vancouver, Victoria, Kootenay Bay and Gulf Islands, Canada, 1989

Mexico City, Mexico - Art & Anthropological Museums, Palenque – Mayan Ruins, 1989

Trip to Mexico: Oaxaca - Ruins of Monte Alban, Mitla, Yagul. Palenque's Mayan Ruins, Bonampak - the sister ruins of Palenque, and Mexico City, 1990

Southwest Ruins- Canyon de Chelly, Oak Creek Canyon, and Sedona, 1990

Southwest Ruins- Acoma Pueblo, Mesa Verde, and Chaco Canyon, 1991

11-11 Psychic and Initiate tour to Egypt - (date connected to Mayan Calendar Event) Cairo, Giza, Kerdasa, Temples of Abu Simbel, Philae Temple, Dendera, Kom Ombo and Valley of the Kings etc. 1991

Trip to India, New Delhi, Rishikesh, Hardwar, Allahabad, Benares, Bangalore, Kerala, Madurai, 1993

Santa Fe, NM and Sedona, AZ, 1994

Trip to museums and ancient sites of England, 1995

Trip to jungles and volcanoes of Costa Rica, 1996

Moved to Jemez Springs, NM, 1998

Visited art museums in San Francisco twice in 1998

I went to Astrological Conventions and Art Museums in Atlanta, Georgia; Chicago, Ill. Denver, Colorado; Monterey, CA; Anaheim, CA; etc. from 1992-1999

Moved back to Laguna Niguel, CA in 1999

Trip to ruins and art museums of Oaxaca And Mexico City, Mexico, 2001

Trip to Vienna and to Reichenau, Austria to go to art museums and to study the old masters misché technique of using egg tempera and oil paints for a visionary artist's seminar taught by Prof. Philip Rubinov- Jacobson. Stopped in London, England to visit art museums on way home, 2002 and again in 2005.

Trip to Venice, Florence, Sienna & Tuscany Italy to visit art museums and for 2-week Misché Technique Seminar with Prof. Philip Rubinov Jacobson in 2003.

Trip to Munich and Viechtach in Bavaria, Germany. I went to visit art museums and to further study misché technique with Prof. Jacobson. June 2004.

I traveled to Williamstown, Mass. and area. I visited the Clark Art institute, the Norman Rockwell Museum, and Frederic Church's home along the Hudson River, 2004 and 2005.

Trip to visit Paris, France to visit art museums. I painted with a group of plein air artists in Giverny, France in Monet's Gardens and in the surrounding villages guided by Cynthia Britain, 2006.

Then I went to Spain and painted with Visionary and Surreal Artists (Martina Hoffman, Robert Venosa, and other great artists) in Cadaques, Spain, home of Salvador Dali. We had a group show. I visited Museums in the area and in Barcelona. 2006.

Trip to art museums and galleries in New York City. 2007 and 2008

AWAKENING LOVE'S VIBRATIONS

I participated in the New York Art Licensing Show in 2008.

In Eureka Springs, Arkansas, I painted in "egg tempera and oil" technique with Philip R. Jacobson, Cynthia Re Robbins and other great artists. We had a group show in The Space Gallery 2008.

In 2008, I went with my mother and brother to Seattle to visit the art museums and galleries. We went on an Alaska cruise trip. I wanted to experience glaciers for a cave series of paintings.

I went with my sister Ruth to visit Seattle and its Art Museum and galleries, and to explore the San Juan Islands.

In May 2009, after my most loving and adoring cat, Timbu died at age 18, I drove up the Coast of CA, OR, and WA. I visited the de Young Museum in Golden Gate Park. I hiked through Muir Woods, The Trees of Mystery and The Oregon Caves. I was inspired by the Oregon Coastline. I went to Victoria, Salt Springs Island, and Vancouver, Canada I then met up with my artist friend Donna Hanna Chase and her relatives. We took the Rocky Mountain train to Kamloops and to Jaspers. I drove with them from Jasper to Lake Louise, Banff and on to Calgary. We took five days to hike in the gorges, along waterfalls, along lakes, and up glaciers. I fell and sprained my wrist while hiking down some loose stones at Lake Louise. That put a damper on any painting for a few months. However, the beauty of the trip was awesome, inspiring, and electrifying. From the giant redwoods, the vastness of the coastlines, the flowers of Butchart Gardens, and the magic of the Canadian Rockies, I stood in awe of the creations of the divine universe and my art shall transform once again. I drove down through Washington, over to Mt. Hood, through Oregon (the scenic route) and then onto Mt. Shasta. July to Aug 2009.

In 2009, I flew a few times to Rochester, New York to help my family.

I participated in the Art Licensing Expo in Las Vegas, Nevada, June 2010.

I flew to Rochester, New York to reunite with my older sisters, identical twins, who had been adopted out at birth. They had just found each other just three years earlier and had become best of friends. It was a special bonding and reunion for all of my family. Everyone was filled with love and my mom who had almost died a few months earlier was filled with joy. June 21, 2010.

During September 2010, I drove up the California Coastline from Dana Point to Point Reyes to meet with my nephew Chris and my newly met sisters. I spent time in San Francisco.

September 2011, I drove up the California Coastline visiting the Redwoods and art museums, Flew to Rochester, NY.

November 2011, I traveled to Salt Springs, Island, Canada. It had been calling to me. I wrote some of my book there.

January 2013, Trip to Ubud, Bali to tour with Della Burford and paint with Philip Jacobson.

June 2013, Trip to Vancouver, to Victoria and Salt Springs Island, Canada

November 2013, Trip to Sedona, visited Vortex and Archeology Site

February 2014, I taught Painting in Penestanen, Ubud on a tour sponsored by Della Burford, Bali, Participated in an Art show in Karja's Art Gallery

August 2014, I drove from California to hike in Bryce Canyon and Zion in Utah, then to visit parks in Colorado and on to Denver and then Boulder, Colorado to take a fast-drying tempera grass' painting class with Philip Jacobson.

In March 2015, I drove up the California coastline and bought a home in Port Townsend, WA. I moved to Port Townsend in June 2015.

I opened Irene's Visionary Art Gallery from May to August 2016.

In February 2017, I went to Bali, Indonesia, participated in an exhibit and gave a lecture on the misché technique, "egg tempera and oil technique".

In November 2017, I went for three days to New York City to visit all my favorite Art Museums and Galleries and then visited family and friends in Rochester, NY.

In late December 2017 - February 2018, I drove down the Oregon and California coastline and then to Southern CA From there I drove to Phoenix, Scottsdale, and Tempe, AZ. I saw a fantastic Aboriginal Women's Art Exhibit at the Scottsdale Contemporary Art museum. On the way back to Washington, I stopped at the Getty Museum. I hugged the giant Redwood trees in Humboldt, CA. I experienced the magnificence of driving near a herd of Elk along the Oregon Coast.

In June 2018, I visited family and friends in Rochester, New York

Acknowledgments

For this book, I wish to thank a number of people. Gratitude of course goes to everyone in these pages, with whom I shared a memory or two. I also want to thank all those wonderful people who have been a part of my life and are not in this story. I want to re-thank Swami Radha, since transitioned, for planting the seed for me to write this story.

I want to thank Mike Robinson, my final editor, who was able to keep the integrity of my intentions alive in this book. Mike is author of *Skunk Ape Semester* and *The Enigma of Twilight Falls* series.

I want to thank my former second husband, Nandu for gently telling me over our eleven-years journey together to write a book about my art and life. Nandu, under the pseudonym of Amarananda Bhairavan wrote the books, *Kali's Odiyya* and *Medicine of Light*. I learned from his process and dedication for writing his stories.

I want to give thanks to my dearest friend Donna Hanna Chase for her encouragement.

I give thanks to my long ago former-boyfriend Robert for going into his attic to retrieve pictures of our six years of travels together, especially to the various Mayan ruins.

I give thanks to Ron Cohan, my former first husband for proofing and editing my eighth draft. I thank him for his quality critiques and remarks. I appreciated his enthusiasm and encouragement. I also thank his wife Lee, a wonderful artist, who gave me enthusiastic advice.

I give thanks to Ron Figueroa, author of *To Save A Dying Planet: A Spiritual Science Fiction Love Story*, for his encouragement.

I want to thank my friend and teacher of the old master art technique, Philip Rubinov-Jacobson. Philip's book, *Drinking Lightening: Art, Creativity, and Transformation* was an inspiration to me.

Lastly, I'd like to share my thoughts about God, as used in this book. God is love. God is the energetic magnetism and vibration that we know as love. Words that I use for "God" are: Goddess, Divine Mother, Divine Universe, The Supreme Inner Most Self, Sweet Lord, Universal Energy, Love, the Cosmos and more. I believe that Divine Grace surrounds us, permeates us, and in those moments, that our soul calls to it, it is there for us, and we feel it. I believe Divine Grace appears in many forms, shaped by our religious beliefs, culture, family and environment. God to me is everything and nothingness.

Buy Irene's book and E-Book: *Revealing - The Evolution of an Artist's Soul, Book One: A Spiritual Journey Trilogy* at Amazon.com, Barnes & Noble, iTunes, Kobo, and at other retail outlets.

See Irene Vincent's Books and Art at: http://www.irenevincent.com

After enjoying my book, please write a review so you can inspire others and let them know how it benefitted you. I deeply appreciate it.

Questions for You & Book Clubs

Chapter-1 What new activities have you had to muster up courage in order to experience them?
Do you feel any sense of separation within or outside yourself or from others?
What areas of your life do you need to find balance? Are you able to balance work and play (creative time)?

Chapter-2 Talk of missiles has escalated again in our society. Do you think there is a way to stop escalation? What questions dominate your thoughts? Can you redirect your thoughts and focus on new questions? How might that affect you?

Chapter-3 Have you ever envisioned a dream house? In what ways has daydreaming and imagining helped to bring changes to your reality?

Chapter-4 Do you share your life's experiences with friends? Have any red flags popped up for you, regarding your relationships and how did you handle them?

Chapter-5 Have you felt another person's voice and presence emitting loving vibrations?
Do you blame others for where you find yourself at this point in life? Who are you grateful for helping you in your life? Do you feel you are responsible for the actions you take to resolve issues in your life? What do you think Swami Radha meant when she said to *suspend your beliefs*? What do you identify with and what is your investment in your identity? Do you over identify with your personality or are you able to be open to other people's beliefs? What does it mean to identify with your higher self? What do you think about the following statement: Attraction and repulsion are no different from one another? How do you discriminate or think things through on a greater or wider level?
Has anyone planted seeds in your consciousness or encouraged you to do something you hadn't thought you were capable of doing?

Chapter-6 When you read the Divine Light Invocation were you able to visualize the light and feel its energy moving through your body? Did you feel deeply relaxed afterword? How did blessing others this way feel to you?

Chapter-7 How do you resolve issues when the other person doesn't want to?

Chapter-8 Did you ever think that while cooking food, you could imbue it with love or other emotions? Have you tried yoga, tai chi or shamanic journeying? What was your experience? Have you thought about what is your mental or physical pain threshold and how it's connected to a crisis threshold? Do you agree that if you lower your crisis threshold you can get to happiness quicker?

Chapter-9 Did you ever have a reoccurring scary dream? Did you ever figure out what it meant? Or did it keep you from exploring your dreams?

Chapter-10 Do you have some favorite travel places that stimulated your imagination and influenced your life? Have you ever felt different vibrations or energies in ancient churches, temples, or pyramids? Why do you think these vibrations seem to emanate in these areas?

Chapter-11 Have you written down and listened to a dream, letting it give you guidance?

Chapter-12 Have you ever contemplated a word or thought for a long-time period, wondering its meaning? (Words such as truth, judgment, and discrimination etc.)
Have you ever released your tensions and pain through creative dancing?
Have you felt your heart open or close towards another person? What might your life look like if you still held an open heart (empathy) toward someone who had hurt you? What would it feel like to have no doors on your heart and to hold an open heart? Could you resolve issues quicker and with more clarity?

Chapter-13 By learning how an image of a snake holds different meanings for different cultures and religions, does it help to open your mind to what it means to you? Can you see that learning the meanings of symbols that show up in your dreams, art, and images can then trigger your intuition and help you discover your personal meaning?

Chapter-14 Strings of information about our DNA fascinated me with our DNA's connection to our ultimate awakening. First, two snakes intertwining a pole was the symbol for ancient healing. Secondly, a snake in ancient Hindu culture was symbolic of being at the base of our spine and its awakening activated our energetic chakras. Then a possibility that a monk envisioned the geometric rose stain glass window that now modern technology says looks like the cross section of our DNA. From this information and experiences, I intuited that meditation and chanting (a sacred vibration) activated our true self and unlocked our spiritual dimension, which is rightfully ours in our DNA. What are your thoughts?

Chapter-15 Did you ever work heartily upon a project and have it not go your way? Did you start over or transform it in some way?

Chapter-16 What do you do to develop a healthy daily routine? Do you keep a diary or journal of any kind? How does it benefit you? What does the word *self-discipline* mean to you?

Chapter-17 Have you ever thought about something for a long time and then suddenly a thought or vision came to you? Are you aware of the concept that you have masculine and feminine attributes or energies? What meaning does the word *oneness* hold for you?

Chapter-18 Have you traveled to a country where they have sacred shrines at trees and or located in public spaces where you can stop and pray? Have you been to Thailand and if so, what were your experiences?

Chapter-19 When I feel imbalanced by life's events, I remember the story *Good News, Bad news, What's the Difference?* Can you see this story helping you and the people you tell it to?

Chapter-20 Are you beginning to see how studying symbols and making art with them can mirror attributes that we might want to integrate into our character and activate in our inner selves?

Chapter-21 Sitting quietly in an ancient ruin surrounded by a vast jungle opened my heart and imagination. Where have you experienced these feelings?

Chapter-22 It was weird because I had so wished that I could have stayed longer at Tikal, so I could feel the land and its ancient energy more deeply and perhaps, have a vision. After I arrived home, I became extremely sick and had the lucid healing dream that connected me with the shaman and his tribe. What are your thoughts on what brought the dream to me? Have you been healed in a dream or felt that you may have helped or healed someone in your dream? Are you open to this being possible?

Chapter-23 Have you traveled to Machu Picchu? What was your experience of it? What are your musings about the origins of the Nazca Lines?

Chapter-24 Have you thought about how you deal with grief? What was your experience? What did you do to overcome grief?

Chapter-25 Have you ever had a healer or shaman heal you of chronic pain with just energy emanating from their hands? Have you ever tried dancing or stretching gently through your pains?

Chapter-26 Sometimes patterns or cycles appear in our life? It was interesting when the astrologer helped me to recognize a pattern in my life? Are you aware of any reoccurring themes in your life? Has an astrologer ever given you guidance?

Chapter-27 What are your processes for relaxing after a stressful work day? Do you value being peaceful?

Chapter-28 In Karl Wolfe's class we contemplated a Tarot card for a week. Its symbolism created a focus of thought from which we could contemplate aspects of our self and life. What is your experience in using symbolic card decks? Within a group, experimenting with different awareness techniques helps to mirror back our experiences, intensifying them? Have you been in any experimental groups for self-awareness? What techniques helped you the most?

Chapter-29 Have you read any of Joseph Campbell's mythic stories? Did they inspire you and your dreaming? Could you relate to any of my dream lessons?

Chapter-30 Have you felt the presence of someone before they arrived to your house? Have you felt waves of bliss from another person walking by you? Have you felt psychic rapport with anyone or with your pets? Do you have friends that stimulate your higher, spiritual thoughts?

Chapter-31 Are you able to see a loved one's life from their need to explore life and grow in a way to be a benefit to themselves and others?

Chapter-32 Have you ever tried to save a relationship through therapy? Are you able to suspend your opinions, or at least stay in peace, when someone else has opposing views? Have you had inspirational dreams during a difficult time?

Chapter-33 In Oaxaca, during the traditional "Breaking of Plates" ceremony, people break their plates and pottery to mark the end of the current year's worries and to bring the dawn of a happy and prosperous New Year. Do you feel that rituals to end things and start afresh are helpful? Have you felt different energies or get different feelings from places and sites? Have you had to release a friend? How did you do it?

Chapter-34 History books are written by people who want to persuade us, and or, use their imaginations to fill in the blanks. Do you feel that traveling can help you get a better view of history or at least stimulate your own imagination? By understanding that everything is made up of vibrating atoms, does that help you to understand that everything has a vibration? In reality, do you think you can sensitize yourself to feel finer and finer vibrations?

Chapter-35 What does the phrase "alchemical marriage" mean to you? In what ways have you or are you ready to explore raising your awareness? Has your understanding of art, symbols, dreams, and visions changed in any way from reading this story?

After reading *Awakening Love's Vibrations*, please go to my Amazon page or where you purchased the book, and write a review so you can inspire others and let them know how it benefitted you, what insights you may have received, and what you enjoyed or didn't like about it. I deeply appreciate it.

Also, you can purchase Irene Vincent's other book: *Revealing - The Evolution of an Artist's Soul, Book One: A Spiritual Journey Trilogy* at: Amazon.com, Barnes & Noble, iTunes, Kobo, and at other retail outlets.

See Irene Vincent's Mystical, Visionary and Shamanic Paintings: http://www.irenevincent.com
See Irene's YouTube Channel: http://www.youtube.com/user/artistvincent/videos
See Irene's artwork on clothing, etc. https://www.cafepress.com/ivincentmysticboutique
Join Irene's Facebook Page: https://www.facebook.com/artist.irene.vincent
Follow Irene on Twitter: https://twitter.com/#!/IreneVincent
Irene's Blog: http://irenesmysticalmoments.blogspot.com/
Please contact me with any questions or share your thoughts at irenevincent3@gmail.com.

If you enjoyed my story, please ask your local library to order it for you, so it will be available for others.

So much love! Thanks, Irene!

www.ingramcontent.com/pod-product-compliance
Lightning Source LLC
Chambersburg PA
CBHW060513300426
44112CB00017B/2649